"Each river has

its own distinct

recipe for water."

ANNE MICHAELS

Meeru Dhalwala & Vikram Vij

VIJ'S AT HOME

RELAX, HONEY

DOUGLAS & MCINTYRE

D&M PUBLISHERS INC.

Vancouver/Toronto/Berkeley

Douglas & McIntyre
An imprint of D&M Publishers Inc.
2323 Quebec Street, Suite 201
Vancouver BC Canada V5T 4S7
www.douglas-mcintyre.com

Cataloguing data available from Library and Archives Canada
ISBN 978-1-55365-572-5 (pbk.)
ISBN 978-1-55365-824-5 (ebook)

Editing by Lucy Kenward
Copy editing by Iva Cheung
Cover and text design by Naomi MacDougall
Photography by John Sherlock
Printed and bound in Canada by Friesens
Text printed on FSC-certified, acid-free paper
Distributed in the U.S. by Publishers Group West

We gratefully acknowledge the financial support of the Canada Council for the Arts,
the British Columbia Arts Council, the Province of British Columbia through
the Book Publishing Tax Credit and the Government of Canada through the
Canada Book Fund for our publishing activities.

Mixed Sources
Cert no. SW-COC-001271
© 1996 FSC
FSC

Introduction

One Sunday evening before writing this book, we sat down with a bottle of wine and the goal of reflecting on what we wanted to write, why we wanted to write and just how much we wanted to share about our home. Instead we stared at one another in wonderment that, after almost fifteen years, we have managed to stay married, work together and still have fun together. Meeru wanted to turn the evening into a reflective therapy session, but Vikram said, "Relax, honey, and just enjoy right now."

"Relax, honey" has been our phrase of survival. It's our cue to each other that "All is fine and I still love you" or, in many cases, "I'm not mad at you anymore." We don't throw around this phrase carelessly—whichever one of us says it is the one who will take responsibility to help the other relax. That particular Sunday evening Vikram cooked dinner and made sure to include lots of vegetables in the lamb stew so that Meeru could actually relax with the knowledge that everyone was getting enough vitamins and fibre. (If Meeru had said "Relax, honey," she would have made the lamb stew with lots of cream and potatoes for Vikram and served the vegetables on the side.)

Days or weeks will go by when neither Meeru nor Vikram has uttered the words "Relax, honey," and the entire family knows that we're working and functioning but not necessarily enjoying one another's company. Sometimes, Meeru will wait for Vikram to say it first and Vikram will wait for Meeru, because neither of us wants to take the first step and make the effort. In such ruts, dinner is what always breaks the ice—Meeru (or Vikram) will have come up with a brand-new recipe and is so excited to share it that she'll say the words as he walks into the kitchen—"Relax, honey. I made a really cool dinner tonight."

For the first thirteen years of our marriage, we didn't have a proper place to eat as a family. Our actual dining room served as a combination of Meeru's office and a playroom so that she could work and be with our daughters, Nanaki and Shanik. The kitchen was crowded. There, we had an invisible, grey table for four, which exuded convenience but no leisure whatsoever. Although we always had Sunday- or Monday-night family meals, on most other nights Meeru would feed the girls an earlier dinner, and then she and Vikram would eat later. We also didn't feel too guilty leaving that table and taking our dinner to the sofa in front of the television.

When we had dinner parties, either we would go through the hassle of emptying our kitchen and bringing in folding bridge tables and chairs (and

covering them with tablecloths) or we would just ask our guests to eat with their plates on their laps. Usually there were pre-party marital arguments because Vikram always wanted to use Meeru's desk as the dining table and Meeru pushed for people to use their laps.

Finally, two things happened. First, in the summer of 2007, Anthony Bourdain's office phoned Vikram, telling him that they wanted to shoot part of the Vancouver episode of *No Reservations,* Bourdain's culinary travel television show, at our home, with the featured Vancouver chefs eating and chatting around our dining table. It seems fair to assume that a chef would have a dining room. For an hour after Vikram informed them that we had no dining room and a crowded kitchen, he decided that this was all Meeru's fault. Meeru snapped back that we weren't going to ruin our family set-up just for the sake of a TV show.

Second and most important, Nanaki and Shanik (12½ and 10) were growing up and no longer needed a playroom or needed their mom to be near while she worked. They were also getting homework and discovering the joys of pop TV and music. The important toys went up to their bedrooms; Meeru's desk and files also went upstairs into an alcove in the hallway, and we had an empty dining room.

So, we had a life-changing moment in the spring of 2008. We set up a dining room in our home and bought a dining table and chairs for eight people. To make this endeavour even more eventful, we spent beyond our savings and bought a dining set that was beautiful to look at and as comforting as a picnic table with duvet seats. We decided that after so many years without a proper eating space, and being in the food business, if there was one thing on which we could splurge, it was our dining room. We went all out and had sideboards, shelves and cupboards built into the room.

To sum up our personalities when it comes to food, it's simple: Vikram is robust, while Meeru is thoughtful. This is how each of us shops, cooks and eats. To turn our crowded kitchen into a leisurely cooking place and to furnish a dining room in a way that reflected our complementary—yet sometimes clashing—traits was a treat. We felt like a newly married couple shopping for our new home. We would sneak out from the restaurants while the girls were at school and go dining-room shopping.

One day they came home from school to find the new family dining table, with two beaming parents showing off their latest joint achievement. What they didn't realize at the time, while they stared at one another smiling as if they had crazy parents, was that our family culture was about to change dramatically.

Vikram started waking up early—although he often doesn't get home until 11 p.m.—to set the table and make breakfast for everyone. For the first time we started eating breakfast together. To make this experience more pleasing to Vikram's eye, he bought various lovely table runners to set the mood. And although in retrospect this sounds crazy, Meeru started spending more time grooming Nanaki and Shanik's hair and helping them choose outfits. Nicely dressed children added to our ambience-driven pleasure. Of course, after a few weeks the girls decided that enough was enough and took over their own hair and clothes. But they continued to wake up earlier so that we could all spend a half hour together in the mornings.

Once breakfast became a new routine, we automatically kept coming up with new ways to make the experience even better than the day before. The joy of breakfast became a reality that was worth the initial investment of waking up earlier. Meeru started making granola from scratch. Vikram began cooking the Indian omelets from his childhood, which included white brioche lightly fried in a pan instead of our regular whole-grain toast.

Of course, not everything stayed perfect. Nanaki and Meeru wanted the richer whole-grain bread, and they wanted it toasted then spread with cold butter straight from the fridge. Vikram insisted that his butter-fried bread was the same as our North American toasted and buttered bread. He was also adamant that the taste of brioche was appropriate for breakfast while the heartier breads were for dinners and soups.

In our pre-dining table family, this difference of opinions would have escalated into a full-on argument that would have covered everything from whose mother knew more about food to Meeru's being a health-freak dictator to Vikram's being obsessed with white bread and meat, and so on. Nanaki and Shanik would have rolled their eyes and gone to school, and we would have spent another hour finishing the argument and making up and then starting the day much later than necessary.

However, the prospect of ruining this new family breakfast around our cherished dining table was unacceptable. We quickly settled on a locally made Italian ciabatta bread, with Vikram's and Shanik's being fried and Nanaki's and Meeru's being toasted. Eventually, Shanik decided that Papa's omelets were good but had too many ingredients in them. Nanaki decided that the family granola had too many nuts and seeds in it and not enough cinnamon. Our cleared-out, updated kitchen has a cooking island, which makes cooking with the girls easier than ever. Now Shanik makes various versions of eggs, and Nanaki has become an expert at mixing granola with lots of cinnamon and maple syrup and very few nuts.

From breakfast we moved on to weekend lunches. Sushi Saturdays gave way to various versions of pressure-cooked organic beans and rice pilaf. Vikram took responsibility for the rice (again, the pilafs from his childhood), and Meeru took care of the bean curries. During farmers' market season, the beans are replaced by whatever vegetables we buy there.

Our dinner routine also changed. Rather than cooking for the girls, Meeru started cooking *with* the girls and sitting down with them for a proper meal at the dining table. Vikram discovered candles in a big way and before he went to work made sure that they were set for our dinnertime enjoyment. As the girls tuned into the fact that they had our full attention around the dining table, they started pitching in to help. We pushed back dinnertime to 8 p.m., and Vikram started coming home early on Tuesdays to join us towards the end. For a restaurant family, three family dinners a week is a big deal.

A rewarding, yet difficult, aspect of our marriage is that we work together and carry the stress of running two restaurants—Vij's and Rangoli—together. At the end of the day it's difficult not to talk or argue about work when two very strong-minded people who always think they are right actually live together. So, unlike breakfast, which revolves around all the wonderful and traumatic stories about school and friends, dinners are often about the wonderful and traumatic issues related to food and the restaurants.

Vikram and Meeru still have heated discussions, but now they are discussions as a family, with full debate, rather than a husband and wife bickering. We spend hours at the table (often with the girls) discussing anything from the carbon footprint of lamb from New Zealand to the merits of buying local versus organic. We have spent days discussing the meaning of "gourmet." We still haven't reached any consensus on this one: is gourmet an extravagant beef tenderloin with a shiitake mushroom and rapini curry, or is it a rustic peasant-style stew? We do agree on one thing: any meal cooked from raw, unprocessed ingredients that tastes good and is served with love is basically gourmet.

Vikram's gourmet comes out when he's cooking curried rack of lamb for dinner parties with our friends. Meeru's gourmet comes out when she empties the grocery bag onto the kitchen island and sees all the colours of the fruits and vegetables, along with purple onions, green onions and garlic. For her the smell of green tomato vines right where they meet the tomato is better than any perfume.

After years of not realizing what we were missing, the arrival of a dining table was like a balm to our lives. We've always loved cooking, but now our rewards are multiplied with the joys of being able to have friends over for dinner without any stress of rearranging kitchens and carrying folding tables and chairs. Simply put, we are less lonely with the freedom of being able to more often invite people over for a meal.

Nevertheless, we simply can't cook like a team, and we finally accept that. One of us has to take the lead, with the other one in a support role. Vikram in his robust mood will spend the day before a party planning and shopping and then cook all day of the party. The two hours before our friends are to arrive have become a family joke—Papa will start yelling about cleaning up the house and setting the dining table. This can't be just any setting—every detail must be looked after in a very five-star way. It's truly a high-maintenance feast with millions of pots and pans, different glasses for each type of wine, and different bowls, plates and cutlery for each food item.

Meeru is most comfortable when she's cooking daily meals for the family or when she's with her staff in one of the restaurant kitchens. When there's no stress, she feels free to experiment and try new combinations of ingredients and spices. When cooking for friends, she enjoys making the meal as simple as possible, with a focus on few dinner items and minimal set-up and clean-up. She also loves to cook in the presence of friends and get their help along the way. Although she often makes a meat curry, she has no qualms about serving a completely vegetarian meal. And she always balances the dishes with little to no fibre with high-fibre dishes.

With the new dining table Meeru often has casual, small dinner parties, which Vikram joins later in the evening when he gets home from the restaurants. No matter how tired he is, Vikram always notices that something is "missing" from the table or that people are pouring their own wines instead of being served. Within minutes, he loosens up and starts drinking and eating, contending with the fact that, just as she'll always be five minutes late, Meeru will never host a fine-dining dinner party on her own.

And this leads us to our cookbook. Almost everything we cook at home for our dining table ends up at either Vij's or Rangoli, our two restaurants in Vancouver. Whereas Vij's is sophisticated and exotic, Rangoli is bright and playful. At the restaurants we'll pair up various dishes prepared at different times. At home we keep it mostly simple, unless it's Vikram's turn to cook.

In this book we've arranged the recipes according to the main ingredients. Traditionally, home-cooked Indian food is served in the middle of the dining table, and people help themselves to what they want and as much as they want. Indian food at home is rarely plated in advance. Whereas some people plate their own food in phases (Vikram's dad will always help himself to a small serving of lentils before anything else), others (like Vikram) will pile everything on their plate at once. You can pretty much make any of these recipes and serve several dishes together or just cook one dish and serve it as your main meal. The combinations are endless, and we've given food-pairing suggestions at the end of each recipe to help you.

Ours is a whimsical, loud and very social cuisine that practically begs you to share it with as many people as possible. Its aromas will go through your entire home, the floor of your apartment building or your entire neighbourhood block. Meeru remembers childhood picnics at the Washington Monument and recalls how non-Indians would often follow the smell of the curry and ask her parents what they were eating. Every time, Meeru's parents would invite the inquisitors to try the food. They always had more than enough, since Indian food tastes even better as leftovers.

We don't have a 100 per cent cooking success rate at home. Many factors— a stressful day that is difficult to shake off, endless errands that still need to be done or just the feeling of not wanting to do any more work—can contribute to a less than perfect meal. But we don't regard cooking as a household chore that can be postponed or neglected. Cooking, just like singing a goodnight song to your child no matter how tired you are, or listening to your sibling's most recent emotional trauma no matter how distracted you are, is one of humankind's unique forms of nurturing. Nurturing takes effort, but it isn't a chore. We believe that when you look at cooking this way, the effort to cook a good meal becomes a form of pleasure and satisfaction.

IN THE KITCHEN

Indian Spices

The point of this cookbook is, for the most part, to show you how to cook easy Indian recipes. Your spice cupboard can play a role in just how easy the cooking will be. In each recipe we have listed the spices that aren't crucial as "optional," but they will really enhance the flavour of the dish if you've got them. If there is a recipe with several optional spices, remember that the more spices you exclude, the simpler the recipe will taste. For example, if there are four optional spices in a recipe, you can exclude anywhere from one to all four spices. In our view, as long as *simple* is still satisfying, the dish is still worth making. After all, daily meals aren't supposed to be complex, unless you enjoy spending lots of time cooking. Daily cooking should be painless and relaxing, and practice will make it easier.

Another option is to roast and grind your own spices. Doing so is time consuming, and it makes no sense unless you cook Indian food regularly. However, it *will* make a difference to the flavour of your dish. We do roast and grind our spices, both at home and at work, but then again, this is our profession. If you don't have the time or inclination, don't fret, because many Indians don't roast their own spices either. If you wish to do so, the most important spices are cumin and coriander (page 40).

Below are descriptions of the spices, in order of importance, that we use in most of our recipes in this book:

Turmeric There are very few recipes in which we don't use turmeric as the basis for our curry, as this spice gives the curry its yellow colour and has an important musky flavour. Almost as important as its taste are turmeric's healthy properties. In India it's not considered a cure-all but a prevent-all: our own families' folklore tells us that turmeric prevents senility, depression and every organ-related cancer. So cook with it every day.

Actually, if you don't mind the smell, turmeric is also great for distressed skin. Mix a couple of tablespoons with body oil for a powerful rub, then massage away. (It's better when someone else does the massaging for at least fifteen minutes.) Traditionally, an Indian bridegroom's bachelor party consists of all the women in his life (mom, sisters, cousins, aunts) giving him a good body rubdown of turmeric. This still happens in India and in Vancouver in some Punjabi families. The idea of the turmeric rubdown is to share the romantic anticipation with the groom and make his skin smooth and sexy for his bride. It's also meant as a final good-luck ritual.

Cumin seeds, whole and ground Next to turmeric, cumin is the most widely used spice throughout India. Cumin seeds give a milder flavour than ground cumin. The seeds need to be sautéed in cooking oil, on their own, in order to cook through. Otherwise you will get a raw taste and the irritating texture of the seeds in your curry.

Coriander, ground Coriander is the seed form of cilantro. Although it is milder than cumin, you don't always need as much, because too much coriander can leave a lingering and overpowering (almost dirt-like) taste in your curry.

Cayenne pepper, red Almost everyone associates heat with Indian food, and with good reason. Although heat isn't at all necessary for a good curry, most people enjoy varying degrees of it. We use a little ground or crushed (you can always substitute one for the other) cayenne in just about everything. We add less when we're cooking for our daughters or Vikram's parents and more when we're cooking for our friends. There is no such thing as too much cayenne for Meeru's parents, and her father is on the verge of eating it straight from the bottle. We consider the spice level in most of the recipes here to be medium, but adjust the level of heat to your own preference.

Garam masala See recipe page 41. There are many, many recipes for making garam masala, which is a northern Indian spice mixture. Cinnamon and cloves are two predominant flavours in most garam masala. We also use the seeds from black cardamom pods in ours. If you don't want to make your own, there are many brands from which to choose.

Below are the other spices that add the famous layers to Indian cooking. Although we encourage you to use as many as possible, they can be optional in many recipes:

Ajwain seeds Often referred to as Indian thyme, ajwain seeds are tiny, yet very strongly flavoured. You don't need to use very much of this spice—just a little adds a lovely taste when it is appropriate to the recipe. Ajwain seeds are also used to help cure and prevent sinus-related problems. Our parents boil ajwain seeds in water and then use the water for their tea. You can also add honey to the water and drink it while inhaling as much of the steam as possible. Our kitchen staff drinks ajwain tea each morning during the winter. Ground ajwain seeds also aid digestion. On days when they are coming up with recipes for new menus and have tasted too much food,

Black cardamom pods and seeds

Meeru and the kitchen staff often mix a half teaspoon each of ground ajwain and ground cumin and a touch of asafoetida and drink it down with some water.

Asafoetida This is a strong spice that is used in minuscule amounts (a small box of asafoetida will last you months). Don't let its pungent, sulphuric smell fool you; when used sparingly, it tastes quite mild and pleasant. Along with turmeric, the medicinal benefits of asafoetida are legendary among the older generation of Indians, and Meeru tends to believe in them—for one thing, it helps calm an upset stomach and eases digestion. Although we don't include it in many recipes, asafoetida can be used in just about any vegetarian dish. Just sprinkle in a quarter teaspoon towards the end of sautéing your onions and/or garlic and allow the spice to sizzle for thirty seconds in the oil. Add any other spices after you have cooked the asafoetida in oil.

Cardamom, black This is an eccentric spice, and for this reason alone it's Meeru's favourite. Black cardamom pods look like crickets and have a much stronger, earthy taste than the smaller, green cardamom. It's very difficult to explain in words the flavour of black cardamom seeds, which are beautiful and hidden beneath an unattractive shell. The best thing to do is to invest the few dollars and buy a small bag. Lightly pound the pod, and peel it back to take out the lovely, moist dark-brown seeds inside. If the seeds are dry and not sticky, then you've got an older pod and you won't get as strong an aroma, so try another pod. Smell the seeds and let us know if you come up with a much-deserved poetic description of the aroma.

When using black cardamom in our garam masala, we shell the seeds and discard the outer pods. (The key to our garam masala is that we use just the seeds of black cardamom, taking the time to shell them.) When adding black cardamom to our basmati rice pilaf, we lightly pound the entire pod and add it to the water and rice during cooking but remove it before serving. Although, like asafoetida, we don't include black cardamom in many recipes, you can use one or two lightly pounded pods in most dishes that don't already have garam masala in them. Don't substitute black and green cardamom for one another.

Cardamom, green Green cardamom is used mostly for chai (Indian tea) and desserts, and many Indians chew on a pod as a breath freshener. The pods and seeds have a flavour similar to fennel but more refined. Green cardamom is much more expensive than black cardamom.

Cinnamon Used in many savoury Indian dishes, cinnamon adds a warm and mildly sweet accent. Because ground cinnamon can overpower a curry, we prefer to use cinnamon sticks and remove them from the dish before serving. We do, however, use ground cinnamon in our garam masala.

Cloves Along with cinnamon, cloves are a main component of our garam masala. We use whole cloves and take them out of the dish at the end of cooking, depending on who is eating. Most Indians don't mind biting into cloves.

Curry leaves In India curry leaves are so common that many vegetable vendors give them away for free with any purchase. They aren't as easy to purchase in North America, but you can find them at most Indian grocers. These leaves are exactly what they're called: they add a "curry" flavour to your dish. Either add them to your boiling curry and allow them to simmer or fry them first in oil before adding your onion, garlic, tomatoes or other ingredients. Because they contain some water, curry leaves can splatter when you place them in hot oil, so keep your head away from the pan. They are hard to chew, so we take most of them out before serving. You can add curry leaves to any dish as you would cilantro, and you can add them with or without cilantro. Regardless, be sure to buy fresh, green leaves and smell them first—if you don't get the curry aroma from the leaves, they won't impart any flavour in your curry.

Fennel seeds We roast our fennel seeds for a few minutes before using them for cooking. This process brings out their anise-like flavour and gets rid of their grassy texture.

Fenugreek leaves, dried green Dried green fenugreek leaves add a flavour similar to that of celery, and they taste great in cream- or yogurt-based curries or meat curries. Sprinkle the leaves into the curry at the very end of cooking. In Indian stores, be sure to buy *kasuri methi*. (Kasur is a northern region famous for its fenugreek, and *methi* is the Hindi and Punjabi word for fenugreek.) Fresh green fenugreek leaves are slightly bitter and are a very popular leafy vegetable in the Punjab, where they are usually cooked with potatoes.

Fenugreek seeds, ground These small yellow seeds provide the "curry" flavour that many people associate with curry powders; however, too much of it can make a curry bitter, so follow the recommended amount of this spice in each recipe. Ground fenugreek can be difficult to find, so we place the seeds in our spice (or coffee) grinder at home and grind our own. Don't confuse these seeds with the leaves, as the two have completely different flavours.

Kalonji seeds Also known as nigella, these small charcoal-coloured seeds give a toasted onion taste to your curry. You don't need to roast kalonji seeds prior to cooking with them, but you do need to sizzle them in oil as you do with cumin seeds.

Kokum A tropical fruit that looks like a dark plum, kokum grows on a tree that is found throughout southern coastal India. You can't eat the fruit fresh from the tree, but the rind of the kokum fruit is semi-dried and used as a spice much like tamarind to add a tart, salty taste to a dish. Although the spice is semi-dried, it is sold as "wet kokum" or "wet black kokum" at Indian markets. In southern India, many drinks are made from kokum because it is known to have many medicinal benefits, including internal cleansing and re-energizing properties (especially important in summer).

Mace This spice is made from the covering of the nutmeg seed. We use ground mace as an optional spice in our garam masala; it's a strong-flavoured spice with a slight anise-like aroma. Do not substitute nutmeg for mace, because the flavours are different.

Kokum

Mango powder This powder is made from unripe, green sundried mangoes. Mango powder gives a tangy and slightly sweet flavour to a curry. In India it's very common to sprinkle a combination of salt, mango powder, black pepper and lemon over regular fruits, such as chopped apples, pears and/or bananas. This fruit *chaat* is a popular street food and is very easy to make at home as well. Mango powder can be clumpy, so be sure to break the clumps with a spoon or with your fingers before using it.

Mexican chili powder Although you can buy this chili powder at various levels of heat, we use *only* mild Mexican chili powder, since we get our heat from either red cayenne peppers or jalapeño peppers. This chili powder goes well with many Indian curries, and you can add it to most of the meat curries in addition to the other spices as you would paprika. Some chili powders have paprika and cumin in them, and we try to avoid these. The best type with Indian food is the Mexican chili powder made from mild ancho chilies.

Nutmeg Available fresh or ground, nutmeg is a spice we use in our garam masala only. We use it sparingly as it has a strong flavour that we find doesn't match with many other spices.

Panch poran This spice blend, which has a deliciously pungent aroma, consists of fenugreek seeds, kalonji, fennel seeds, yellow or black mustard seeds, and cumin seeds. It is usually sold as premixed whole seeds. You can grind the seeds in your spice (or coffee) grinder (no need to roast them, but you can if you want to bring out that extra flavour). Whether ground or whole, panch poran should be cooked (or sizzled) in hot oil for thirty seconds (if ground) to forty-five seconds (if left as whole seeds) before anything else is added; otherwise the raw pungency of the spices remains in the curry.

Panch poran is the Bengali equivalent of the Punjabi garam masala, not in terms of its flavour but in terms of its reflecting the tastes of the people and their cuisine. Although we don't use this spice as extensively as we do garam masala, feel free to experiment with many of the ingredients for recipes in this book by using only panch poran, turmeric (which goes with any Indian spices or mixtures), red cayenne pepper and salt. In many dishes, we find that panch poran tends to be a stand-alone spice mixture; in other words, to flavour your curry, all you need is just the right amount of this spice.

Paprika We use paprika mostly for aesthetic reasons, but it does offer a very mild taste that complements turmeric. When cooking a simple dish, paprika comes in handy, since most households have it. The more spices you add in a curry, the less you need paprika, unless it's strictly for the colour.

Pomegranate seeds, ground In this book we use ground pomegranate seeds (known as *anardana* in Hindi) as an optional spice to add a sweet-tart component to the curry. You can buy ground anardana in most Indian stores. Do not try to grind your own pomegranate seeds in your spice (or coffee) grinder, as they are very sticky and will burn out the motor or gum up the blades.

Saffron Used mostly in rice pilafs with nuts and raisins or in Indian desserts, saffron is so delicate, yet subliminally strong, that most other spices will either hide its taste or clash with it completely. As a result we don't use very many other spices when cooking with saffron. Finding the right combination of spices for saffron isn't easy, but once we figure out a recipe, it's never difficult and makes for a very different and elegant curry. We use turmeric as the background spice and green fenugreek leaves as the accompanying spice. Turmeric nurtures the saffron, while fenugreek adds more dazzle. For some heat, red cayenne pepper matches saffron perfectly. The heat from jalapeño peppers or black pepper, however, clashes with saffron.

It's difficult to write down a measurement for saffron, because the amount you use depends on the quality of the saffron you buy. As fragrant as saffron can be if used in the right amounts, your dish will become bitter if you use too much. If the threads are deep red with a strong aroma, then you won't need too many. If there are orange threads mixed in with the deeper red ones, you will need more. Saffron also loses its lustre the longer you store it, so buy the smallest amount you can, unless you will be cooking with it often. Indian saffron is harvested by hand in Pampore, Kashmir, in the first few weeks of November, just as it has been for the past two thousand years. It is considered to be among the best in the world (and also among the most expensive), but in North America we usually hear only about Iranian or Spanish saffron, perhaps because Kashmiri saffron isn't readily available here.

Star anise Although star anise comes from China and Southeast Asia and is not an Indian spice, we like its combination of sweet, pungent and licorice flavours. It isn't essential by any means to Indian cooking, but you can try to use small amounts of star anise instead of cinnamon in your cooking, or add it to your rice pilaf. Note that it is not as forgiving as cinnamon if you use too much.

Sumac Used mostly in Middle Eastern and Turkish cooking, ground sumac is reddish and looks like ground pomegranate seeds or even some forms of paprika. It has a very mild, yet acidic, flavour and is often sprinkled on kebobs, pilafs and warm salads. You don't need to cook ground sumac—just sprinkle it on your food at the end of cooking. You can also sprinkle ground sumac into plain yogurt with some salt, then add grated cucumber or carrots to make *raita*, a side dish for cooling your palate.

Tamarind This sturdy, drought-resistant tree's pods grow in clusters and contain seeds that are surrounded by a tart pulp. The raw pulp is formed into cakes and sold in Indian markets. It's important to boil and strain the tamarind pulp to make a smooth, tart paste (page 42) without the seeds. It is added (in small amounts) to give slight acidity to curries or used to make chutneys.

Indian Staple Ingredients

Beans, kidney Only two dishes in Indian cuisine use kidney beans, but these two dishes are so common and popular that Indians probably buy more kidney beans than the rest of the world combined. One is called *rajma chawal* (kidney beans and rice), and each particular cuisine within India must have its own recipe for it. We give our family recipe in this book (page 114). In the second dish, kidney beans are combined with whole urad lentils to make a Punjabi lentil curry. This is also the basis of the rich and velvety *dal mukhani*, which is served at many northern Indian restaurants.

Beans, navy These small, mild-tasting, white beans aren't Indian in origin and are rarely used in India, but they are readily available in North America and taste great in lighter Indian curries. White navy beans are also higher in iron and fibre than kidney beans or chickpeas.

Breads Traditionally, Indians eat *chapatti* with their daily meals. Chapatti is a round flatbread made from a combination of wheat, bran and all-purpose flour. There are hundreds of such combinations, depending on the brand of chapatti flour. For a treat or when dining out, *naan* is very popular. Naan is a thicker, heavier flatbread made from all-purpose flour, eggs, buttermilk and oil. In North America you can easily buy ready-to-eat chapatti and naan. However, you can easily substitute any wheat flatbreads for chapatti and pita bread (sort of) for naan. We also enjoy substituting a fresh baguette in place of chapatti or naan.

Chickpea flour Chickpea flour is an important and common food in northern India. We use it for many vegetarian dishes and, most importantly, we use it for pakoras (page 124), the deep-fried spicy vegetable fritters. It is also used as a thickener in curries. Although in North America chickpea flour is considered to be a substitute for wheat or refined flour, in India we simply prefer to cook with it for its special taste. Many Punjabi street foods and desserts have chickpea flour in them. Chickpea flour is usually made from black chickpeas, which are indigenous to northern India.

Chickpeas, black These dark chickpeas are regarded as being better than the regular white chickpeas in terms of nutritional value. In the villages of many of our kitchen staff members, black chickpeas are fed to horses and buffaloes to strengthen them. (In addition to being versatile work animals, buffaloes produce about one half of the milk consumed in India.) In fact, in Hindi and Punjabi the word used most often to describe the benefits of black chickpeas is *thakut,* which means "strength." We grew up hearing about how they strengthen the body and the mind. Our moms made sure that we drank all the soup stock from the black chickpeas as well.

You can pretty much substitute black chickpeas in place of white ones in most curries. Just remember that they aren't available in cans and that you will need to soak them for six hours and then use the same water you soaked them in for the curry. When Meeru comes up with a recipe that requires just the black chickpeas and no water, the kitchen staff always saves the water the black chickpeas soaked in for use in another curry. They say that throwing away that water is like throwing away a health tonic.

Coconut milk and coconut cream Northern Indian cuisine doesn't use much coconut milk or coconut cream, and neither is considered an important ingredient by any means. However, this is not so for the rest of India. Most notably, coconut plays a big role in Goan and southern Indian cuisine. We have often incorporated coconut into our recipes and find that, although northern Indian recipes mostly call for yogurt or whipping cream, you can just as easily replace these with coconut milk or coconut cream. Coconut milk is used in the saucy curries and should always be stirred before using, since the coconut cream often separates from its water. Coconut cream is used in drier curries.

Ghee This is clarified butter, and you can cook with ghee instead of cooking oil for any recipe. The butter is gently boiled, and the whey and other milk solids are scooped out with a sieve and discarded as they rise to the top. You will be left with golden ghee. Although the thought of ghee frightens many health-conscious people, its status as an indicator of wealth as well as its health benefits (in small quantities) are legendary in India. You can also heat ghee to a very high temperature without changing its chemical properties—in fact, you can even deep fry in ghee. We often use ghee when cooking Indian food and believe that, when used in moderation, it is healthier than other oils.

Lentils, mung or moong Whole green lentils, often labelled as mung beans, are available at any grocery store. In Indian cuisine, these are called whole moong lentils and they aren't used as much as split moong lentils (the green lentils are just halved) or split, washed moong lentils (the green lentils are halved and their skins removed, which makes them very quick-cooking yellow lentils). We cook with all three types of moong. Moong lentils are a favourite in the Vij parents' household.

Lentils, toor These yellow lentils are quick cooking and are used mostly in southern Indian cooking. They are larger and heartier than split, washed moong lentils.

Lentils, urad These lentils look identical to whole moong lentils except that they are black. They take much longer to cook but hold their texture even after hours of cooking. They are a staple for making *dal mukhani* (a velvety, rich northern Indian lentil dish available at many Indian restaurants). Like moong lentils, urad lentils are also available as split urad lentils and split, washed urad lentils. Urad lentils are a favourite in the Dhalwala parents' household.

Rice, basmati In Meeru's view, brown basmati is as good as white basmati with many curries. Brown rice, including brown basmati, is a whole grain and is high in B vitamins, iron, healthy fatty acids and fibre. As with white basmati, we suggest that you stick with Indian- or Pakistani-grown brown rice, since *basmati* is a special aroma and texture that comes with the Himalayan soil and water. If you can't find the Indian brown basmati variety, use any regular long-grain brown rice.

Many people associate the nuttier taste and firmer texture of brown rice with super-healthy, yet plain-tasting, vegetarian food. However, the reason many people don't like brown rice usually isn't because of the rice itself but either because of a lack of flavour in the dish accompanying the rice or because the brown rice grain has not been properly cooked, resulting in a heavy and porridge-like sludge. See page 55 for our recipe. Especially if you are using many spices and ingredients, brown rice works wonders in a risotto-style pilaf. Brown rice pilafs aren't as dry and flaky as traditional pilafs, but they are nevertheless delicious.

Sugar, raw Known as *gur,* this is an unprocessed Indian brown sugar that is golden, moist and smooth (it does clump up, though). It is often called "jaggery," but we have learned that true jaggery, which is usually in nugget form, isn't of the same quality as pure raw sugar, and we avoid it. Pure raw sugar tastes very rich, and we prefer to use it for all of our desserts. It is also delicious on its own, and our Vij's and Rangoli kitchen staff eat about a half teaspoon per person after lunch every day to sweeten their palate after a spicy meal. If you cannot find Indian raw sugar, you can substitute *panela,* which is a raw sugar made from sugar cane and is sold in many Latin grocery stores.

Cooking Oils

In our previous cookbook, *Vij's: Elegant and Inspired Indian Cuisine*, we specified canola oil or ghee (clarified butter) in each of our recipes. We aren't married to either, so in this book we have merely written "cooking oil" in our recipes. We encourage you to use whichever oil you prefer, although we don't suggest margarine or cooking sprays, since they aren't naturally derived and we also question their claims to being healthy or low-fat.

For sautéing at home, we usually use between one-third to a half a cup of oil per six servings. However, we've specified a third of a cup of oil for most recipes. So, if you're watching your fat consumption, we hope you'll use this lesser amount of oil rather than substituting margarine or cooking sprays. If you're less concerned about your fat intake, add a bit more oil, if necessary.

The subject of cooking oils is widely discussed on the Internet and in research papers. As with all food products, there is a lot of controversy over which oils are the best for our health, whether or not the hexane found in many non-organic oils is harmful to our health, and what environmental impacts result from genetically modified oils. People seem to have many different notions (based on a whole variety of facts) about which oil is best. For example, we have read in respectable journals about the health perils of mustard oil (used predominantly and widely throughout northern India) and also about the unmatchable health benefits of mustard oil. The same goes with coconut oil (used predominantly and widely throughout southern India). We do know for sure, though, that both oils are excellent for hair and body massages and surpass any commercially available hair conditioners.

At home we cook with many different oils, believing that's the best strategy for health and variety. Among the ones we use most often are extra-virgin olive oil, non-GMO organic canola oil, grapeseed oil and ghee or butter. Because we hail from northern India and grew up with its taste, we do enjoy cold-pressed mustard oil, but it is very difficult (and expensive) to buy in Canada.

Pressure Cookers

Meeru bought an inexpensive pressure cooker for the first time in 1997, when she wanted to save time yet make healthy foods for her then-toddler, Nanaki. The cooker sat in its box for ten days. Once out of its box, it sat on the counter for a month. Like many people, Meeru was intimidated by the look of the pot and the thought that she might accidentally misuse the pressure cooker and cause its contents to explode.

A pressure cooker reduces cooking times and is the exact opposite of a slow cooker, or Crock-Pot, which simmers food all day or night until it is ready to eat. We find that slow cookers don't always work with Indian food because sautéing onions, garlic and spices is such an important part of the cooking process and you can't do this in a slow cooker. With a pressure cooker, however, sautéing is easy. After you sauté the onion, garlic, tomatoes and the spices, the uncooked food is placed in the cooker with water, then covered by a lid with a tight-fitting seal. The cooker is set on high heat until it reaches full pressure, at which point you reduce the heat slightly and the pressure cooker releases steam through a small regulator or gasket at regular intervals. Because the pressure inside the pot is maintained at a much higher level than in a conventional pot, the food cooks up to ten times as fast. Then, once you turn off the cooker, the lid will not open until the steam has decreased to a safe pressure, so you'll need to wait for it to cool.

In India pressure cookers are so common that nobody gives them a second thought. Most people buy their beans and lentils in bulk, and the main meat

is goat, which takes a long time to cook. Cooking gas is scarce and very expensive, so the drastic reduction in cooking time with a pressure cooker is a must. In North America these same benefits apply. When using a pressure cooker, you can eat healthier and save money on organic foods. For example, organic stewing meats are cheaper than more premium organic cuts, and using bulk organic chickpeas, pinto and navy beans and brown rice is less expensive than cooking with canned varieties or buying smaller quantities. You save time and energy (gas or electricity) by using a pressure cooker. You also save your house from smelling like curry, since the spices do not permeate the air for hours. (Smelling curry when you're hungry is a different experience from smelling curry while you're snuggling into bed with a book.)

We use the pressure cooker with many of these recipes, but you will need to experiment to find which uses work best with your schedule and food preferences. As an example, rather than soaking bulk chickpeas overnight and then boiling them for an hour, you can cook them to perfection in a pressure cooker within twenty-five minutes. You can make any stewed meat curry—goat, beef, lamb and pork—in this cookbook in a pressure cooker. It takes over an hour to cook meats with the regular stovetop method but only five to ten minutes in a pressure cooker. You can sauté your onion/garlic/tomato masala in the pressure cooker and then add the beans or meats, so you don't have to deal with any extra dirty pans. (Follow the guidelines that come with your pressure cooker and then adjust your own cooking from there. We don't have a set amount of water that we add for our bean and meat curries, for example, because we sometimes like them to have lots of sauce and sometimes less, but we always follow the recommended measurement for brown rice.)

There are many excellent-quality pressure cookers, European and Indian, for sale, but we are familiar only with the Indian pressure cooker and we use the Hawkins brand. We recommend that you go online and do some research to find a model that suits your own needs. Although the European cookers tend to be more expensive, they may have certain qualities that you prefer. Ours is a five-litre stainless steel cooker; it cost us seventy dollars, and we've had it for years. *When we give pressure-cooking times in this book, they are based on the amount of time it takes our cooker, which is an older model.* Newer and different models may take different amounts of time or water.

Although the cookers may look or seem intimidating, they are very simple to use, especially after you take a quick look through their manuals. If you can use a cellphone, you can use a pressure cooker.

Guidelines for Easier Indian Cooking

To make it simple, remember the following rules whenever you cook
from this book.

1. A masala *means a mixture of spices, either dry or wet.* A dry masala consists
   of the dry spice mixtures—for example, a garam masala. A wet masala is the
   mixture of the dry spices with tomatoes, onions, garlic, etc. The wet masala is
   the basis for your curry, and when we talk about "the masala sticking to the
   bottom of the pan" we are referring to the wet masala. You don't want to burn
   your wet masala.

2. *Keep turmeric, cumin seeds, ground cumin and ground coriander in
   your cupboard at all times.* You can do wonders with just these spices for your
   dry masala.

3. *The preparation and cooking times are estimates, and you can often use
   the cooking time to do other tasks.* How long it takes you to make a recipe
   will depend on how fast you chop onions, garlic and tomatoes. Vikram is way
   faster than Meeru, so we've used Meeru's cooking time as the time estimate.
   Our estimates cover the complete cooking time, including simmering time,
   so if the recipe calls for a meat to simmer for an hour, you can use that time
   to prepare another dish, sit down with a glass of wine or do many other
   non-cooking-related tasks.

4. *Cook a batch of rice—brown or white—while you prepare your dinner.*
   Plain rice—brown or white—will go with just about every recipe, even if we
   have recommended a baguette, naan or chapatti to go with the dish.

5. *Nearly every recipe can be modified according to your preferences.* For most
   recipes, you don't need every ingredient, so don't shrug off a dish just because
   you don't have a certain vegetable or spice. At all times, feel free to substitute
   any personal preferences or adjust the quantities of various ingredients, such
   as using less water because you prefer a less soupy curry or less onion because
   you or other family members don't like a strong onion taste. (For the longest
   time Nanaki kept saying that she didn't like Indian food. After lots of trial
   and error Meeru finally figured out that it was the taste of cumin that Nanaki
   didn't like. Now, whenever Meeru makes a curry with only small amounts
   of cumin, Nanaki happily eats Indian.) Similarly, don't stress over measurements, unless we specifically state in the recipe that you should be exact.
   At home we never use measurements.

6. *Sizzle your seeds.* Cumin, kalonji and mustard seeds need to sizzle in a bit of oil in order to cook through. (Think of sizzling as swimming—if the water [oil] is too shallow, you can't swim. You don't need ten feet of water to swim, but swimming in a wading pool isn't easy either.) Depending on the heat of your stove, it will take anywhere from thirty seconds to two minutes for the oil to heat up enough to sizzle the small seeds. Some ground spices, such as asafoetida and panch poran, also need to sizzle in oil in order to cook through. Ground spices will take from twenty to thirty seconds to cook.

7. *A good tomato flavour makes a good curry.* If fresh tomatoes are not very good quality and/or too expensive, use canned, unsalted tomatoes. Dead, pale tomatoes will give you a dead, pale curry. If your tomatoes are very juicy, you may end up with a more liquid curry, but this is not a problem in terms of taste.

8. *Salt enhances the flavour.* Because of all the spices, Indian food tastes better with a bit more salt in comparison with other cuisines. If you are watching your salt intake, please make your own adjustments to the amounts we have suggested. Remember, home-cooked food often has way less sodium than takeout, packaged or canned foods. We often switch back and forth from sea salt to table salt, and we find that sea salt tastes less "salty."

9. *Stove temperatures will vary from unit to unit, so watch your heat.* Commercial stoves burn much hotter than the average home stove. For some of the recipes, Meeru used her sister's small kitchen with a gas stove in New York City. If the numbers go from 0 to 8 on your stove, on a large-diameter burner 8 is high and 6 to 7 is medium-high. The numbers 4 and 5 are medium and 1 is simmer. Remember that the diameter of your stove burner will also have an effect on your cooking time: the smaller the diameter, the longer it will take, especially if you are cooking large amounts in large pots. Some electric stoves also take longer to cook.

10. *Be creative and design your own recipes.* Once you've made a few of our dishes, you may want to experiment with your own variations. Here are some general ratios for cooking a meal for six people that you can use when trying to come up with your own Indian curries:

⅓ to ½ cup cooking oil (page 26)

1 medium or large onion, chopped

3 to 6 medium cloves garlic, chopped

1 cup chopped tomato (or ½ cup if you prefer a less soupy, less tangy curry)

1 tsp turmeric

½ to 1 Tbsp salt

11. *Don't be afraid to cook in large batches.* All curries taste great as left-overs. Unless we specifically mention in a recipe that a dish will not keep, you can refrigerate leftovers in an airtight container for up to one week.

12. *Mix and match your dishes.* Indians serve many dishes all together, all at the same time. Our "serve with" suggestions are just a few of many dishes that might go well with the recipe you're making, but feel free to serve it on its own or with any other dish that appeals to you. In a few places, we've noted if a particular flavour really will not complement the dish, so you can avoid those combinations; for example, the saffron in the Rice Pilaf with Cashews, Cran-berries and Saffron clashes with the jalapeño peppers in such dishes as the Red Bell Pepper and Shallot Curry or the Grilled Marinated Wild Salmon in Green Onion, Coconut and Ginger Broth.

Wine Pairings with Indian Food

We drink wine almost every night, regardless of the type of meal we're having. Even when the pairing with spicy food isn't technically great, we still enjoy ourselves. There are plenty of wine books out there for those who want to really learn their wines. Here, Mike Bernardo, our general manager and wine director, and Vikram, who is a certified sommelier, offer their accumulated tidbits of wine information, considerations and ideas in relation to Indian food.

An obvious consideration when pairing wines with Indian food is the heat that comes from either red cayenne pepper or jalapeño peppers. After that there are the layers of spicing, ranging from mild to strong. Finally there is the non-spice ingredient that plays a large role in choosing wines: the cream, coconut, yogurt or tomato base of the curry.

Mike keeps a wine fridge in his thousand-square-foot condominium and owns over six hundred bottles of wine, ranging from $15 to $1000 per bottle. He doesn't have a daily budget; what he drinks depends on what he's eating, and he has no problems opening a $100 bottle of wine at 11 p.m. after work.

Wine is a very personal taste. I have some regular customers who come in and drink only Super Tuscan wines because that is what they enjoy, no matter what they are eating. Although there are many guidelines for pairing wines, the final decision is based on your personal palate.

My first piece of advice is to *stay clear of wines with a high alcohol imbalance.* This isn't necessarily about the percentage given on the bottle. It's more about how well the other flavours balance with the alcohol content. You can't tell from looking at a bottle of wine what the alcohol balance will be like, unless you're familiar with the wine or the style of wines from particular winemakers, so it's best to ask the specialist at the wine shop if you don't know. For example, some Portuguese reds from the Douro region or some Shiraz from Australia have a high percentage of alcohol per volume but taste smooth and balanced. With wines that have a strong alcohol presence, you risk feeling a burning sensation in the esophagus or upper chest with spicy foods.

Select wines with a balance of sweetness and some acidity. These will complement and soothe the spices.

Avoid white wines with a high oak content or with rich buttery flavours (i.e., certain types of Chardonnays) *as well as white wines with a strong grassy flavour* (i.e., certain Sauvignon Blancs). These wines set up the same burning sensation as spicy foods and will seem to intensify the heat from the food. Don't avoid Chardonnays altogether though, because those with a tropical fruit note or Chablis style work really well with our food. As for Sauvignon Blancs, some of the best pairings with Indian foods come from this varietal—you just want to select one with more earthy tones.

Select red wines that are fruit forward and low in tannins. By fruit forward I mean wines that start out with plum or berry flavours when you sip them. High tannins also clash with the strong spices, so look for the more aged wines, where chances are that the tannins have had time to soften.

In my view there's no such thing as recommending, say, Chianti or Gamay to go with Indian food—the differences are huge within each varietal. One wine producer's methods and winemaking style and technique will vary greatly from another's, as will the growing conditions and soil from country to country, so you can have two Gamay wines that taste very different.

If there is one region with higher odds of producing a wine to go with Indian food, I think it's the Rhone Valley, whose appellations include Côtes du Rhône, Côte-Rôtie, Hermitage, Saint-Joseph, Gigondas, Châteauneuf-du-Pape, among others. The wine-producing areas of the Rhone Valley are divided into north and south, and there is variety in the type of grapes and quality of wines. Generally speaking, wines from this region tend to be softer on the tannins and more fruit forward in taste, especially the older ones.

This doesn't mean that I think the best wines for pairing with Indian food come only from the Rhone Valley. I'm suggesting that it's your best bet if you enjoy red wine in general but aren't too familiar with all its nuances.

If you truly want to play it safe or don't know the wine preferences or tastes of your guests, *sparkling wine* (I do prefer the taste of Champagne, although it's pricey) *or German Riesling always tastes good with Indian food.* Serve these wines at any time during the meal.

Vikram keeps many wines for years, to open on special occasions. For our daily drinking, we keep our budget to under $25, with no budget for special occasions.

Some Indian dishes, such as the Yogurt Curry on page 92 or the Oven-baked Spicy Brussels Sprouts Crumble and Sour Cream Curry on page 88, you just can't pair with wine. In these cases, *select wines that you just enjoy* no matter what. I tend to choose my wine on its own merits rather than pairing it with Indian food. Whereas I thoroughly enjoy bigger, more intense red wines, Meeru sometimes doesn't and she claims that I'm trying to burn her chest with huge wines and huge spices.

I don't have a favourite style, since I love any well-made red wine and I sometimes don't want my food to interfere with the type of wine I'm in the mood to drink. I think any varietal can go with Indian food, depending on the winemaker and his or her style of wine. If you do wish to pair a wine with Indian food, generally the bigger red wines, such as some New World Syrahs (Shiraz) and Cabernet Sauvignons, Bordeaux and Chianti wines, are a bit trickier—the pairing is not always a match made in heaven, but it's worth pursuing if you love such wines, which I do. Depending on how big these wines taste in terms of their sweetness and alcohol balance, they don't always match spicy Indian food as well as they would match, say, cheese, prosciutto or steak. But there's no rule that you must swoosh down your food with a sip of wine. I take a bite of my dinner, wait and then have a sip of my wine. I let each one stand on its own.

If you are a swoosher-downer, then in my view your best bet is to stick with a German-style Riesling or an Austrian white such as Grüner Veltliner. These wines have enough sweetness and are slightly acidic and dry, which in turn balances the spice in Indian food. Because these wines are so easy to drink with spicy foods, I find it very easy to get drunk on them as well. I do prefer an off-dry white wine rather than one that begins and ends with sweetness. A sweet white wine from beginning to finish, when combined with strong Indian spices, is too rich for my palate.

I strongly recommend that you *try out wines from your local winemakers*, if there is a wine industry in your area. If you're in California, this is a no-brainer, and the Pacific Northwest has emerged as a very strong wine region, as has the Niagara region in Ontario. I think Oregon has some of the best Pinot Noirs to pair with Indian food. British Columbia has some world-class white wines (Chenin Blanc, Gewürztraminer and Ehrenfelser are among the best) and excellent red wines.

While in Virginia visiting Meeru's parents, we often drink Virginian white wines. While visiting Cape Town, we thoroughly enjoyed local reds and whites from the Stellenbosch region (Syrah and Chenin Blanc stand out). When in New York visiting Meeru's sister, we have enjoyed some New York red wines. In Bombay we always drink Indian red or white wines; they are very

new in comparison with wines from other wine-producing regions of
the world.

Newer winemaking regions especially need local support if they are ever
to become expert winemaking regions. On weekends visit wineries and offer
your opinions and critiques. Whether we are winemakers or restaurateurs,
the sincere feedback from within our own community is crucial in terms of
improving the quality of our product and boosting our confidence. (Although
the compliments feed my confidence, it's the candid comments and suggestions from our customers that keep us on track with tweaking, fixing and
improving our food and service.)

Remember that growing grapes and keeping vineyards for winemaking are agricultural acts; they involve decisions about what goes into the soil
where the grapes are grown, what is or isn't sprayed on the grapes, and how
and how much to irrigate the vines, etc. Many wineries are increasingly using
sustainable farming practices and including this information on their labels.
After the harvest comes the winemaking process, and each winemaker has his
or her techniques for pressing, aging and bottling their product—the details
of which are becoming important considerations for the consumer. When
you visit a winery, you can ask about the farming and winemaking processes
directly.

So, for me, drinking a glass of wine is about much more than popping the
cork and considering it as a complement to my meal. I'm intrigued and inter-
ested by everything it took to create the wine, from the quality of its grapes
to the artistry of its making. The work that goes into producing a great bottle
of wine is right up there with the effort that goes into making a great meal,
and the end results of both are equally satisfying.

CONDIMENTS & COMPLEMENTS

No INDIAN MEAL is complete without at least a chutney or pickle or a piece of bread or some rice. These are the dishes we call our condiments and complements.

In India there are hundreds, if not thousands, of types of chutneys (and pickles) to go with Indian food. The point of the chutneys in this book is to give quick and simple foods, such as oven-baked chicken breast, seared tofu and noodles, more depth. We've included in the following pages some of our own ideas and recipes, which are also useful to add extra flavour to main dishes or to spruce up leftovers at lunchtime. Freeze chutneys in small, sealed containers and thaw them when needed.

When we were younger, our moms used to make tiffin lunches for our dads. A tiffin is a four- or five-piece stainless steel lunch box that holds various curries, rice and/or Indian bread. Just as we have bicycle couriers in North America, India has a bustling industry of *tiffinwalas*, or tiffin couriers, who deliver hot lunches from homes to offices. One of the most common lunch-making "tricks" is to combine whatever little curry is left over from last night's dinner with some rice.

We took the leftover lunch concept one step further and came up with some fresh and easy vegetarian sautés that you can add to just about anything—rice, toast, couscous, boiled potatoes—to turn plain food into a flavourful meal. We also like to add sautés to various curries as a final touch. Although they aren't necessary, they complement so many foods that you may find yourself combining them with dishes you would otherwise have tossed because you didn't know what to do with them.

Roasted Whole Cumin and Coriander

MAKES 1 CUP
roasted whole or ground
cumin and ¾ cup
roasted ground coriander

PREP & COOKING TIME
5 minutes + 20 minutes to cool

Cumin

1 cup cumin seeds

Coriander

1 cup coriander seeds

You can sift and roast cumin and coriander seeds and store them, separately, in airtight containers. Just grind the seeds in your spice (or coffee) grinder prior to cooking. If you buy these seeds in bulk bags, it's important to quickly sift through the seeds for small pieces of dirt and rocks.

As a gauge for the ratio, one tablespoon of whole cumin seeds will yield one tablespoon of ground cumin. Two tablespoons of coriander seeds will yield a tablespoon and a half of ground coriander. Grind the roasted spices as you need them, or grind them all and store them in an airtight container.

Cumin Heat a 10-inch heavy-bottomed frying pan on medium-high for 1 minute. Add cumin seeds, and, stirring regularly, cook for 3 to 4 minutes, or until darkened. Pour roasted seeds onto a plate and allow to cool for 20 minutes. Grind the seeds, if desired. Store whole seeds in an airtight container in a dark cupboard or drawer for up to 9 months or ground seeds for up to 6 months.

Coriander Heat a 10-inch heavy-bottomed frying pan on medium-high for 1 minute. Add coriander seeds, and, stirring regularly, cook for 3 to 4 minutes, or until seeds look slightly burned on one side. Pour roasted seeds onto a plate and allow to cool for 20 minutes. Grind the seeds, if desired. Store whole seeds in an airtight container in a dark cupboard or drawer for up to 6 months or ground seeds for up to 3 months. In our view, coriander becomes stale faster than cumin.

Garam Masala

MAKES ½ CUP

PREP & COOKING TIME
10 minutes + 20 minutes to cool

1 heaping tsp whole cloves

1½ tsp black cardamom seeds (from about 10 whole cardamom pods)

6 Tbsp cumin seeds

1 Tbsp pounded cinnamon sticks

¼ tsp ground mace (optional)

¼ tsp ground nutmeg

WE use our own signature recipe at home and at our Vij's and Rangoli restaurants. Garam masala is a warm spice mixture used in northern India. Its main components are cumin, cinnamon and cloves, and we add nutmeg and the seeds from black cardamom pods. Using mace is an option, but be careful not to overdo it because too much mace can ruin an entire batch.

For a long time we were religious about telling people to make their own garam masala at home. The spices should be sifted (this ensures that pieces of dirt and stones aren't ground into the powder), roasted and cooled prior to grinding. Many store-bought garam masala aren't pre-roasted and, therefore, are not as strong in flavour.

We have changed our tune. Although making garam masala yourself is definitely better, there's nothing wrong with trying out the various brands available at Indian grocery stores, if you don't have the time or inclination to make your own. Basically, there are times when you make your own chicken stock and others when you buy from the market, and the same applies to garam masala. The decision is yours.

Please note, however, that some garam masala are made with coriander, and ours is not. So if a recipe of ours has both coriander and garam masala in it, and the garam masala you're using contains coriander, you may need to use half the coriander called for in the recipe the first time you make it. Then you'll know if you need more coriander the second time around.

Turn on your stovetop exhaust fan. In a heavy-bottomed frying pan, heat cloves, black cardamom seeds, cumin seeds and cinnamon sticks on medium to high, stirring constantly. When cumin seeds darken, 5 to 8 minutes, remove the pan from the stove. Transfer the roasted spices to a bowl and allow to cool for 20 minutes.

Place roasted spices, mace and nutmeg in a spice (or coffee) grinder and grind until the mixture has the consistency of store-bought ground black pepper. Store in an airtight container in a dark cupboard or drawer. Will remain fresh for up to 6 months.

Tamarind Paste

MAKES 1 ¾ CUPS

PREP & COOKING TIME
30 minutes + 30 minutes to cool

2 ½ cups water

14 oz package pure
seedless tamarind *(imli)*

IF you've got the time, we recommend that you make your own tamarind paste using the recipe below. It's pure tamarind and no sugar. For the nights when you're rushed, use one of the various varieties of store-bought tamarind paste, but be careful to buy one that doesn't have too much sugar and that tamarind is the main ingredient!

An alternative to using tamarind paste is to substitute a mixture of four to five fresh, pitted dates chopped finely and mashed together with two tablespoons of fresh lemon juice. Use an amount equivalent to the quantity of tamarind paste called for in the recipe. You won't get a tamarind flavour, but you will get a sweetness and tartness in your dish.

Combine water and tamarind in a small pot and bring to a boil on high heat. Reduce the heat to medium and boil tamarind for 10 minutes, using a spoon to mash and break the tamarind into small pieces. You will notice some hard pieces and sometimes bits of seed that cannot be mashed. Remove the mixture from the stove and allow to cool in the pot for half an hour or until lukewarm.

Place a fine-mesh sieve over a bowl. Strain the tamarind mixture, using your hands or the back of a metal spoon to mash the solids through the sieve and into the bowl, until all that is left are pieces of tough skin. Discard or compost these skins. The resulting paste should have the consistency of puréed baby food.

Will keep refrigerated in an airtight container for 5 days or frozen for up to 3 months.

Sour Cream Indian Dressing

THIS is a rich dip that we use with raw vegetables, in sandwiches and even as a chutney. At Rangoli we serve this dressing with our Spicy Pulled Pork Roast with Garlic (page 201). We prefer regular full-flavoured, full-fat sour cream, but you can use low-fat if you prefer.

In a medium bowl, mix together all of the ingredients. Cover with a lid or plastic wrap and refrigerate the mixture for at least 15 minutes. Will keep refrigerated for up to 1 week.

MAKES 1 CUP

PREP TIME
15 minutes + 15 minutes
of refrigeration

1 cup sour cream

½ tsp salt

½ tsp ground cayenne pepper

1 tsp green fenugreek leaves

½ tsp finely chopped garlic
(1 small-medium clove)

SERVE WITH

Tangy and Spicy
Chopped New Potatoes

Baked Jackfruit in
Garlic Marinade

Spicy Peas and Mashed
Potato Toasted Sandwiches

Spicy Pulled Pork Roast
with Garlic

Apple Chutney

MAKES 3 ½ CUPS

PREP TIME
20 to 30 minutes

2 lbs apples, peeled,
cored and roughly chopped

5 oz red onion
(1 small-medium),
roughly chopped

1 cup fresh mint,
leaves only,
roughly chopped

1 Tbsp salt

2 Tbsp tamarind paste
(page 42)

3 Tbsp demerara sugar
or any brown sugar

½ tsp crushed or ground
cayenne pepper (optional)

SERVE WITH

Any dish, especially meats

MEERU had bought some expensive, organic apples that Shanik informed her were "yucky, soft and sour." Six of them sat in the fruit bowl for days, while Meeru was in denial that no one in the family was going to eat them. Yet she couldn't throw them away.

One time in India, Meeru was eating papaya on the porch and throwing the skins out onto the road for the cows to eat. She had eaten a lot of papaya and threw all her peels out onto the road at once. However, instead of a cow, a little boy came running out of nowhere to examine her peels. Then, as if he had hit the jackpot, he yelled out to other kids. From the porch, Meeru watched five street kids devour the discarded peels, leaving just a paper-thin papaya skin for the cows. The kids knew Meeru was watching, and when they were finished they asked if she always ate fruits like this and said they would come back the next day. They were smiling at her as if she were the most generous person in the world. That was almost twenty years ago. Today Meeru imagines those kids having a heyday in her household compost.

Although she was ready to throw all the apples in the compost bin, she ate one to ease her guilt. While she was chewing, this recipe immediately popped into her head. You really don't have to use mushy apples for this chutney, and if you're a connoisseur of apples, make it with whichever variety you like best. Granny Smith apples make a chutney that's slightly too sour for our taste, but you may like sour. We also prefer the sweet and tart flavour of tamarind paste (page 42) over the sourness of lemon, but if you don't have tamarind, use lemon instead to give a bit of zing to the chutney. For this recipe, use the amount of onion called for in the recipe; too much will overpower the apples. We serve this chutney with just about any Indian dish; it also tastes great in a ham or roast beef sandwich.

In a food processor fitted with a grating attachment or in a blender, combine all ingredients and process until they become a smooth chutney. If you're using a blender, add a few tablespoons of water if necessary to process ingredients smoothly.

Will keep refrigerated in an airtight container for up to 1 week.

Cilantro Chutney

MAKES 2 CUPS

PREP TIME
20 minutes

W E make big batches of this chutney and then freeze it in smaller containers. Whereas the Apple Chutney (page 44) is sweet, this one tastes strongly of raw cilantro. This cilantro chutney tastes great alongside the apple chutney, so go ahead and serve both. Vikram's mom always offers two or three different chutneys when she has friends over for tea and savoury snacks. Cilantro chutney also tastes great in a cucumber sandwich made with white bread.

Cilantro and mint are the two most common ingredients used in Indian green chutneys, and there are many versions of green chutney throughout India. Although the kokum isn't a crucial ingredient in this chutney, it really does add a nice salty, sour flavour. You'll find it readily available in the spice section of Indian grocery stores, where it will be labelled as "wet black kokum" even though it looks much like a dried black plum. You may need to remove some seeds before using the kokum, and because it is moist you will need to pack it down when you measure it. Use the amount of onion specified in the recipe, as any more will overwhelm the chutney.

Spread out the kokum and quickly remove and discard any hard seeds. Chop the skins, pack as many of them as will fit into 1 Tbsp for this recipe and set aside.

In a blender or food processor, combine all of the ingredients. Process until you have a smooth chutney.

Will keep refrigerated in an airtight container for up to 10 days or frozen for up to 3 months.

¾ oz kokum (optional)

2 bunches cilantro
(11 to 12 oz cilantro),
roughly chopped

1 Tbsp ground cumin

1½ tsp salt

½ tsp black pepper

1 small jalapeño
pepper, chopped

½ tsp ground cayenne pepper

2 Tbsp fresh lemon juice

1 tsp asafoetida (optional)

2 Tbsp chopped garlic
(6 medium cloves)

5 oz red onion
(1 small-medium), chopped

1 Tbsp ground sumac

¾ cup water

SERVE WITH

Any other dish in this book

Tomato and Onion Chutney

THIS chutney is so versatile that we make big batches of it and always keep some in our fridge at home. Nanaki doesn't like ginger or jalapeño, so sometimes we make it without these two ingredients, but then Meeru and Vikram don't enjoy it as much. We prefer to eat this chutney warm, but you can serve it straight from the fridge.

You can eat this chutney with almost anything. Once after returning home from vacation to an empty fridge, we boiled some pasta and mixed in this chutney as we would pesto. We use this chutney in sandwiches and as a stir-fry paste for sautéing vegetables. We also spread the chutney over grilled steaks, pork tenderloin and even over oven-roasted chicken, especially when we're drinking red wine.

In a medium pot, heat oil on medium-high for 45 seconds. Add onions and sauté for 8 minutes, or until dark brown but not burned. Stir in tomatoes, ginger and jalapeño pepper and sauté for 3 to 4 minutes. Add lemon juice, salt and sugar, stir and sauté for 2 minutes, then remove from the heat.

Will keep refrigerated in an airtight container for up to 10 days.

MAKES 2 CUPS

PREP & COOKING TIME
40 minutes

⅓ cup cooking oil

3 cups finely chopped onions (2 medium-large)

2 cups finely chopped tomatoes (4 medium-large)

4 Tbsp chopped ginger (optional)

3 Tbsp chopped jalapeño pepper (optional)

⅓ cup fresh lemon juice

2 tsp salt

3 Tbsp sugar

SERVE WITH

Brown Basmati and Portobello Mushroom Pilaf

Mushroom and Celery Root Basmati Rice Pilaf

Black Chickpea Pakoras

Butter Chicken Schnitzel (as a replacement for the homestyle butter sauce)

Beef Short Ribs in Light Cumin Broth

Any plain grilled or seared meats, including hamburgers

< *clockwise from top left: Apple Chutney, page 44; Tomato and Onion Chutney; Tamarind Chutney, page 49; Cilantro Chutney, page 45; Sour Cream Indian Dressing, page 43*

Apple-cilantro Chutney

MAKES 2 CUPS

PREP & COOKING TIME
20 minutes + 25 minutes
to roast and grind fennel seeds

6 Tbsp fennel seeds

1 bunch cilantro (5 to 6 oz),
washed, destemmed
and roughly chopped

3 Granny Smith apples, cored,
peeled and roughly chopped

¼ cup fresh lemon juice

¼ cup plain yogurt
(minimum 2% milk fat)

1½ tsp salt

1 Tbsp ground cumin

½ medium jalapeño
pepper (optional)

SERVE WITH

Pork Tenderloin with
Glazed Oranges
(as a replacement for
the glazed oranges)

Any seared or grilled meats,
including pork chops, lamb
chops, steak or lamb tenderloin

MOST Indian restaurants showcase a green curry, and Vikram has always loved the contrast of bright green cilantro or mint with the earthy colours of the other curries on the table. Green chutney in India is like applesauce in North America; it is very common. This recipe brings green chutney and applesauce together.

The chutney in this recipe was developed specifically to go with seared or grilled meats, especially when you're drinking white wines. The more cilantro stems you use, the more you'll detect a slight bitterness in contrast to the apple. If you don't like this flavour, then be sure to cut off most of the cilantro stems.

Heat a 10-inch heavy-bottomed frying pan on high for 1 minute. Add fennel seeds, and, stirring regularly, cook for 2 to 3 minutes, or until slightly darker. Pour roasted seeds onto a plate and allow to cool for 20 minutes. Grind the fennel seeds in spice (or coffee) grinder. Set aside 1 Tbsp of the ground fennel seeds for this recipe and store the rest in an airtight container in a dark cupboard or drawer for use in other dishes.

In a food processor, combine cilantro, apples, lemon juice, yogurt, salt, cumin, ground fennel seeds and jalapeño pepper and pulse to a smooth chutney. Spoon chutney into a bowl, cover and refrigerate until serving.

Will keep refrigerated, covered, for at least one week, so you can store leftovers or make it in advance.

Tamarind Chutney

I F you have made tamarind paste (page 42) for a specific recipe, you can always make this chutney with the leftover tamarind. It's tart and sweet and a bit savoury from the salt and cumin. Because it's so flavourful on its own, you don't need very much—try it with Indian snacks such as samosas or pakoras, as a spread in a Cheddar cheese sandwich or as an addition to a fruit salad (without citrus fruits). The best thing to do is to taste it and then get creative. Meeru can even imagine this chutney as a funky steak sauce.

If you really like this tart and sweet flavour, you can also make a drink from the chutney: just stir one or two tablespoons of chutney into one cup of water and add some ice. You can even finish it with some mint leaves and/or a shot of vodka.

Combine all of the ingredients in a small, heavy-bottomed pan. (Start with ½ cup of water. If the mixture is thick like mayonnaise, add the additional ¼ cup. It should have the consistency of ketchup after simmering.) Bring to a boil on medium heat, stir well and simmer for 10 minutes. Turn off the heat and allow to cool for 30 minutes before serving.

Will keep refrigerated in an airtight container for up to 10 days. (We're pretty sure it will keep longer, but we always finish it up before then!)

MAKES ABOUT 1 ¼ CUPS

PREP & COOKING TIME
10 minutes + 30 minutes to cool

1 cup tamarind paste (page 42)

½ to ¾ cup water

½ tsp ground cayenne pepper

1½ tsp salt

7 Tbsp sugar

1 tsp ground cumin

SERVE WITH

Any other dish in this book

Roasted Eggplant Raita

MAKES 3 CUPS

PREP & COOKING TIME
30 minutes + 30 to 45 minutes
to roast eggplant + 1 hour to chill

1 lb whole eggplant
(1 large), skin on

½ tsp cooking oil or more,
for oven roasting

1 tsp cumin seeds

1½ cups plain yogurt
(2 to 4% milk fat)

¼ cup finely chopped
green onions, white
and tender green parts only

½ tsp finely chopped ginger

1 tsp ground coriander

1 tsp salt

½ to 1 tsp finely chopped
jalapeño pepper

½ cup chopped cilantro
or 1 tsp dried mint

SERVE WITH

Vegetable and
Yellow Lentil Curry

Chickpeas in Star
Anise and Date Masala

Prawns in Pomegranate Curry

To obtain the flavour in this dish, you must roast the eggplant. Although this step can seem a bit of a hassle, it is not hard, and the rest of the recipe is also easy to make. Vikram and Meeru have taught Nanaki how to roast eggplant, and this saves us time while we do other things. If you have a gas stove, you can easily roast your eggplant on the burner. If you have an electric stove, you will find this a very messy and almost impossible task, so we recommend that you roast your eggplant in the oven. Use the large purple eggplant rather than the long, thin Japanese eggplant to make this recipe.

Serve this raita, either at room temperature or chilled, as a dip with warm pita bread or naan or as a side dish alongside spicier curries. It also tastes great just mixed in with rice. Use yogurt with 2 to 4 per cent milk fat, since skim-milk yogurt will make a thin, tart dip.

To roast eggplant, use either the stovetop-roasting method (if you have a gas stove) or the oven-roasting method.

For the stovetop method, place eggplant directly on top of the gas burner. Turn the gas on high and don't forget to turn on your exhaust fan. Using a pair of tongs, rotate eggplant every 3 to 4 minutes, for a total of 25 to 30 minutes. The eggplant will make sizzling noises. When eggplant has completely wilted and you think that you won't be able to turn it over (you will, as long as you hold it at its crown), it is roasted. Transfer eggplant to a medium bowl and allow to cool for 10 minutes.

For the oven-roasting method, preheat the oven to 425°F. Poke eggplant 5 or 6 times with a knife. Rub oil on the eggplant, then place it on a baking tray. (This method is messier but faster than wrapping the eggplant in aluminum foil.) Bake for 45 minutes, or until eggplant is shrivelled and appears to be very mushy. Remove from the oven and allow to cool for 10 minutes.

Hold eggplant over a large bowl (in case it slips out of your hands) and run cold water over it. Using your fingers, peel off and discard the burned skin until eggplant looks as clean as possible. Drain any water from the

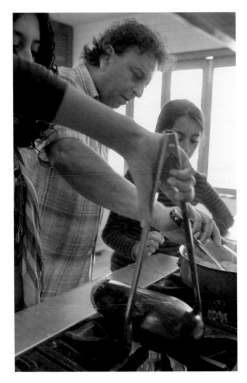 

bowl, then place eggplant in the bowl and mash flesh with a large fork
or finely chop with a knife.

Place cumin seeds in a small frying pan on high heat. Using a wooden
spoon, stir cumin (or grasp the pan handle and lightly shake the frying
pan so that the seeds don't stick) for 1 to 2 minutes, or until dark brown.
Turn off the heat and pour seeds into mashed eggplant.

Add yogurt, green onions, ginger, coriander, salt, jalapeño pepper
and cilantro (or mint). Stir with a spoon, cover with plastic wrap
and refrigerate for at least 1 hour if you wish to serve it chilled.

Will keep refrigerated in an airtight container for 2 to 3 days.

Paneer

MAKES 7 TO 10 OZ,
depending on final
water content

PREP & COOKING TIME
45 minutes (varies from
stove to stove) + at least
30 minutes to set

½ cup water

8 cups whole milk

¼ cup white vinegar
or fresh lemon juice

PANEER is a staple mild Indian cheese made from whole milk. The thought of making paneer at home may seem intimidating, but it is truly an easy, easy cheese to make. It just takes time for the milk to boil. Once you have some paneer in the fridge, it's so healthy and versatile that you can whip up many Indian meals. You can lightly pan-fry cubes of paneer and sprinkle them with lemon, cayenne and salt to serve as an appetizer. You can prepare paneer kebobs to eat in place of meat ones. You can make soft paneer to use as a breakfast cottage cheese. Finally, you can add paneer to enhance just about any vegetable curry or rice pilaf. Nanaki and Shanik's favourite way to eat paneer is on its own, just like a piece of Cheddar cheese. Sometimes, Nanaki even dips the pieces in honey or fruit preserves.

As we make paneer more and more every week, we find it quicker and more manageable to make a small batch from a two-litre (half-gallon) container of milk. Heating a gallon of milk can take a long time on a stove with small burners. Making smaller batches also means that we can use a large, thin cotton handkerchief (an eighteen-inch square) rather than great lengths of cheesecloth to strain the boiled milk. Any thin cotton item works well (Meeru actually cuts up Vikram's old *kurtas* [long Indian cotton tunics]); T-shirts do not, as the material is too thick. You can easily wash a large handkerchief and use it four or five times for paneer; however, if you use regular store-bought cheesecloth, be sure to fold it up several times. (Although doing so makes the cheesecloth more tedious to wash—pieces of cheese really get stuck into the small pores—you will end up with a better paneer.)

The final weight of your paneer will vary depending on how long you allow the water to drain from the cheese. We prefer our cheese slightly firm and slightly soft, and it is on the heavier side. Others may want their paneer firmer and will drain it longer, resulting in a paneer with less weight. Nevertheless, paneer is rich, and, even if a recipe in this book calls for more, you won't notice the difference if you are an ounce or two below the recommended weight. You can always double this recipe, too. We never measure the weight of our homemade paneer and just add what we've made to our recipe.

Pour water into a medium, 8-inch high, heavy-bottomed pot, then add milk. Turn on the heat to medium and wait for milk to start boiling: a commercial stove takes about 15 minutes, our gas stove at home takes 20 minutes, your stove will most likely take from 20 to 35 minutes. Do not stir the milk. As the milk nears the boiling point, watch it very carefully, with vinegar (or lemon juice) in hand. Milk will start to rise in the pot. Once it has risen 3 inches, turn off the heat immediately and gently swirl in—but do not stir in—vinegar (or lemon juice). You want it to go throughout the milk and not just in one spot. Allow the mixture to sit for 10 minutes while the milk solids separate from the liquid.

Place a colander in the sink. Cover it completely with the handkerchief (or folded cheesecloth). Slowly and carefully pour milk into the colander. Allow milk solids (paneer) to sit in the colander for 15 minutes, or until the extra water has drained into the sink. Gently gather the four corners of the handkerchief (or cheesecloth) and tie them together to completely enclose the paneer.

continued overleaf…

Half-fill a medium pot with water. Place the wrapped paneer either in the sink or on the counter right next to the sink (so that water from the paneer can drain directly into sink). Place the pot of water directly on top of the paneer and press it down gently. This will both flatten the paneer and help it release some of its water. Once the pot can easily balance on the paneer, allow it to sit for 15 minutes (for a soft paneer) to 1 hour (for a firmer paneer). Most recipes in this book call for paneer that is medium firm (40 minutes to sit) to firm (1 hour). Soft paneer is meant to be eaten more like a cottage cheese. Our paneer is usually 2 inches thick. Remove the pot, untie the handkerchief (or cheesecloth) and gently slide one hand under the paneer. With your other hand, place a large plate over the paneer and carefully invert them together. Remove the handkerchief (or cheesecloth), gently scraping off any paneer stuck to the material.

Use immediately or keep it refrigerated, tightly sealed in plastic wrap, for up to 5 days.

Brown Basmati Rice

RADITIONALLY Indians don't eat brown basmati rice, as they prefer the more neutral taste of white basmati. For thousands of years, in fact, Indians have been removing the outer brown husk and polishing the brown basmati into white rice. As each layer is removed, so is most of the nutritional value and fibre, but the rice becomes lighter and flakier.

Some people say they find brown rice hard to digest, but Meeru, Nanaki and Shanik eat it two to three times a week and don't notice any digestion issues. Out of habit, Vikram will only eat brown rice if there is no other option, and Meeru often makes sure there isn't one. He always enjoys the brown basmati but still doesn't actively seek it out.

For extra flavour, we sauté onions and add them to the rice. Even if you choose not to use the onions, do add the oil or butter.

Finally, a bonus with brown rice is that you can freeze it for up to a month and the rice doesn't lose its texture once you thaw and reheat it (just add a bit of water to cover the bottom of the pot).

Place rice in a medium bowl, wash well under cold water and drain. Repeat the washing and draining once more, then set rice aside.

In a large pot, melt butter on medium (or heat oil on medium-high for about 1 minute). Add cumin seeds and allow them to sizzle for 15 seconds. Add onion and sauté until browned, about 10 minutes. (The less you sauté the onions, the sweeter they will taste; the more you sauté them, the more they will have a toasty, roasted flavour.)

Add water (or stock) and salt to the pot, then add rice. Using your hands, scrape rice grains from the bowl into the pot. Stir well, increase the heat to high and bring to a boil. Immediately reduce the heat to a simmer, cover and simmer for 45 minutes.

The cooking time for the rice will vary from stove to stove, so remove the lid and check for water. If there is no extra water in the pot, carefully taste the rice to see if it's cooked through. If it's not, put the lid back on, turn off the heat and allow the rice to cook in its steam for another 15 minutes. Or, add ½ cup more water and continue simmering for 10 minutes. If there is still extra water in the pot after 45 minutes, cook rice, covered, for another 10 minutes. Turn off the heat, keep the lid on the pot and allow rice to sit for 5 minutes before serving. If you like your rice firmer, serve it immediately once you have turned off the heat.

SERVES 6 TO 8
as a side dish

PREP & COOKING TIME
15 minutes to sauté the onions + 50 minutes to 1 hour to simmer the rice on the stovetop (or 12 minutes in a pressure cooker)

2 cups brown basmati rice

2 to 3 Tbsp butter or cooking oil

1½ tsp cumin seeds (optional)

1 large onion, finely chopped (optional)

4 cups water or stock (chicken or vegetable)

1 tsp salt

SERVE WITH

Any other dish in this book (except those specifically noted)

Rice Pilaf
with Cashews, Cranberries and Saffron

SERVES 6
as a side dish

PREP & COOKING TIME
45 minutes to 1 hour

1½ cups white basmati rice

2 ½ cups cold water

¾ cup raw unsalted
cashews, roughly chopped

¼ cup cooking oil

1 tsp cumin seeds

1 small onion, finely chopped

1 Tbsp chopped garlic
(3 medium cloves) (optional)

½ tsp turmeric

1 tsp salt

10 to 20 threads saffron (¼ tsp)
soaked in ¼ cup hot water

⅓ cup dried cranberries

ONCE you get the hang of making this pilaf, you can play around with the ingredients. If you wish, use almonds or walnuts in place of cashews, or try dried blueberries or raisins instead of dried cranberries. You can even add sautéed vegetables such as cauliflower or green beans, or a cup of cooked chickpeas or pinto, navy or kidney beans. You will just need to adjust the salt. You can also use your own preferred measurements—if you like fewer nuts and more berries, that's fine. The more of both you use, the healthier the pilaf. For this particular recipe, we recommend that you use only white basmati, because we don't think saffron matches the flavour of the brown rice.

The colour of your saffron water should be more red than orange. If it's orange, try adding more threads. The higher the saffron's quality, the fewer threads you'll need. Dip your finger in the water to test the flavour of the saffron.

This is Vikram's rice recipe, and first soaking the rice for at least 20 minutes and then steaming it at the end, with the lid on, for at least 10 minutes is important. If you choose to use no other ingredients except for the rice, water, oil, cumin, onion and salt, you will have plain basmati rice to serve as a side with any meal. And if you choose not to add saffron, you can double the turmeric for added flavour.

In a large bowl, wash and drain the rice twice in cold water. Add the 2½ cups of cold water to the drained rice and soak for at least 20 minutes and up to 1 hour.

In a small, heavy-bottomed frying pan, heat cashews on medium-high, stirring constantly for 3 to 4 minutes. The tiny pieces will start to burn, but continue stirring until the cashews are light brown with darker brown edges. Turn off the heat and empty cashews into a bowl to cool.

In a medium pot, heat oil on medium for 45 seconds. Add cumin seeds and allow them to sizzle for 15 to 30 seconds. Immediately add onion and sauté until light to medium brown, about 5 minutes. Add garlic and cook for 1 to 2 minutes, or until golden. Add turmeric and stir for 45 seconds, or until a slightly darker shade. Add rice with all of its water and salt. Increase the heat slightly, stir and bring to boil. Stir in the saffron and its water. Reduce the heat to a simmer, cover and allow to cook

for 10 minutes. Without removing the lid, turn off the heat and allow rice to cook in its steam for another 10 minutes. Remove the lid and stir.

Pour cooled nuts and cranberries into cooked rice. If you're adding sautéed vegetables or beans, add them as well. Mix until well combined. Serve immediately.

SERVE WITH

Any other dish in this book

Spinach and Split Pea Mash

SERVES 6 TO 8

PREP & COOKING TIME
45 minutes to 1 hour
+ 2 hours to soak the split peas

1½ cups green split peas

3½ cups water

¼ cup cooking oil or ghee

1 cup finely chopped
onion (1 medium)

1½ Tbsp finely chopped
garlic (4 to 5 medium cloves)

2½ Tbsp or less chopped
jalapeño pepper (1 large)

1 tsp salt

7 to 8 oz fresh spinach
(1 bunch) with stems

1 Tbsp ground sumac

2 tsp dried mint

SERVE WITH

Chicken, Tomato
and Green Bean Curry

Beef Short Ribs in
Light Cumin Broth

Pork Tenderloin with
Glazed Oranges

Any non-Indian dish that
you'd usually serve
with mashed potatoes

WE usually serve this mash with the Pork Tenderloin with Glazed Oranges (page 199), but it would also taste great with lamb, beef or any fish. Since it is a nice (and healthy) alternative to rice or potatoes, you could even add this Indian-spiced mash to non-Indian dishes. One day we had some leftover mash in the fridge and some almost stale bread on the counter. We toasted the bread and spread cold mash on the slices to make delicious split pea mash sandwiches. You don't need to limit yourself to stale, toasted bread, as any bread would be delicious.

Although split peas are usually not soaked, we soak them in this recipe to get the right texture and to reduce the boiling time.

Place split peas in a colander and wash and drain them several times to remove any dirt, rocks and other impurities. Transfer split peas to a medium pot, cover them with the 3½ cups water and soak for 2 hours.

Bring split peas and water to a boil on high heat. Reduce the heat to low, cover and simmer for 15 to 20 minutes. Most of the water should have been absorbed, but the peas should be cooked and moist with a little water still in the pot. Cook longer or drain if there is too much water in the pot. Remove from the heat and allow to cool for 30 minutes.

In a medium frying pan, heat oil (or ghee) on medium-high for 45 seconds. Add onion and sauté for 5 minutes, or until golden. Add garlic and continue to sauté for 2 to 3 minutes, or until golden. Add jalapeño pepper, salt and spinach. Stir well and cook for 1 minute, or until spinach wilts. Set aside to cool for 15 minutes.

Once the split pea and spinach mixtures have cooled, purée each one separately in a food processor. Process split peas until smooth, spinach until roughly puréed and slightly chunky.

In a medium bowl, combine peas and spinach. Stir in sumac and mint. Will keep refrigerated in an airtight container for 4 to 5 days.

Spiced Pistachios and Dates

MAKES 1 CUP

PREP & COOKING TIME
15 to 20 minutes

1 Tbsp butter

1 cup whole unsalted
pistachios, shelled

¼ tsp salt

¼ tsp ground cayenne pepper

1 tsp garam masala (page 41)
or ground cumin

8 oz fresh or dried dates
(11 large or 14–15 medium),
pitted and chopped

SERVE WITH

Any other dish in this book

THIS is a great sweet, spicy and nutty topping for a lighter meat dish, such as chicken or pork. We serve it with the Pork Tenderloin with Glazed Oranges (page 199), but you can serve it even with non-Indian-style meats. We have been going through a bit of a lovefest with dates—their gentle sweetness when combined with spices provides a perfect finish to many dishes.

In a shallow pan, melt butter on medium heat. Add pistachios, stirring often, for 2 minutes. Add salt, cayenne, garam masala (or cumin) and continue to stir for 1 minute. Stir in dates until well combined and cook, stirring constantly, for 2 minutes. Remove from the heat and allow to cool.

Will keep at room temperature in an airtight container for 5 to 7 days. (The nuts taste stale past that time.)

TASTY SAUTÉS

There are cultural words for which we can't find the perfect translation. Just as we have never been able to find the right word in Hindi for "privacy," we haven't found the right word in English for *tharka*. The closest word in English, if we use it as a noun, is "sauté."

With the right tharka, plain lentils suddenly come to life or leftover plain rice becomes a spicy pilaf. In its most elementary form, a tharka is cumin seeds sautéed (or sizzled) in oil and called *jeera ka tharka*. We've taken this basic tharka one step further by adding various vegetables to enhance the taste as well as the look of the dish. We call these quick-cooking recipes our sautés. Serve these toppings over plain lentils or rice, a square of paneer (page 52), your favourite cooked vegetable or a slice of bread. Or serve them as a side dish with a heartier main dish. The sautés are best served immediately.

Beet Greens
Sautéed in Ginger, Lemon and Cumin

SERVES 8

PREP & COOKING TIME
45 minutes

1½ lbs beet greens with stems (about 2 bunches), chopped in ¼-inch pieces

1 lb daikon, red radishes or turnips, peeled and thinly cut into "shoestrings" 2 to 3 inches long

2 Tbsp finely chopped ginger

½ cup fresh lemon juice

4 Tbsp sugar

1 Tbsp salt

2 Tbsp ground cumin

1 tsp ground cayenne pepper (optional)

⅓ cup cooking oil

SERVE WITH

Rice Pilaf with Cashews, Cranberries and Saffron (or the plain white rice version)

Brown Basmati Rice

Ground Lamb, Beef and Lentil Kebobs

Beef Short Ribs in Light Cumin Broth

Grilled Beef Tenderloin with Almonds and Garlic

THIS recipe is delicious made with beet greens, but you can substitute other similar green leaves such as spinach or even collard greens. If you use kale for this recipe it will take longer to cook. Daikon, red radishes (you can even wash and add the radish greens) or turnips are the best partners for beet greens. If you prefer a slightly bitter taste, use the daikon; if you prefer a sweeter taste, use turnips. Be careful not to overcook the turnips, as they will turn mushy and too sweet. Daikon is available at most Indian or Asian grocers.

At Vij's, we were serving various versions of beets but discarding the greens—using them for vegetable stock didn't work in our curries. Finally, we came up with a recipe to use the greens as well. As it turned out, this recipe became even more popular than the beets. The chopped beet greens cook very quickly, so it's important to cut the daikon, radishes or turnips thinly. Serve this sauté piping hot as an appetizer instead of a salad, on top of brown or white rice, or as a side dish to a meat curry.

Place greens and daikon (or radishes or turnips) in a large bowl. Add ginger, lemon juice, sugar, salt, cumin and cayenne and mix well.

Just before serving, heat oil in a wok or large frying pan on high for 30 to 45 seconds. Add vegetable mixture, including all the lemon juice at the bottom of the bowl. Heat greens, stirring regularly, for 4 to 5 minutes. Serve immediately.

Celery, Tomato and Green Onion Sauté

SERVES 6 TO 8

PREP & COOKING TIME
20 minutes

6 to 8 green cardamom
pods (optional)

¼ cup cooking oil

1 cup chopped tomatoes
(2 medium)

½ tsp salt

1 Tbsp mild Mexican
chili powder

½ tsp black pepper

1 lb celery, cut in ½-inch pieces

¾ cup finely chopped
green onions, white and
tender green parts only

SERVE WITH

Any steamed fish

Spice-encrusted Lamb Popsicles

Any of the goat curries

THIS recipe requires very little oil because, despite its name, it is not actually sautéed. The dish has a kick to it, but not a spicy one, unless the Mexican chili powder you buy is spicy. The cardamom pods make this sauté a nice accompaniment to almost any of the oven-cooked meat dishes.

If you don't like celery, use green bell peppers instead. We like our celery cooked yet still crunchy, but if you prefer yours softer, cook it for an extra minute. Be sure to add the green onions at the last minute—if you make this dish ahead of time, add them only after you have reheated the celery. Serve a dollop of this sauté as a topping or as a warm side salad.

With a knife, lightly crack the cardamom pods. With your fingers, peel back the shell to release the seeds and collect them in a small bowl. Discard the shells. With a rolling pin or a mortar and pestle, crush cardamom seeds (or leave them whole if you don't mind biting into them).

Heat oil in a small pot on medium for 1 minute. Add tomatoes, cardamom seeds, salt, chili powder and black pepper. Stir and cook for 1 minute. Add celery and cook for 2 minutes, stirring regularly. Turn off the heat and stir in green onions. Serve immediately.

Red Bell Pepper, Onion and Sumac Sauté

THIS slightly sweet sauté works well with any of the meat dishes in this book. Sumac trees produce a fruit that can be ground into a powder that's most often used in Turkish, Greek and Middle Eastern cooking. It has a mildly tart flavour.

You can buy ground sumac at any Middle Eastern or Greek grocery store, but some Indian grocers do carry it too. Be careful not to confuse sumac with ground pomegranate spice, as they look and taste similar, but pomegranate is too strong for this dish. We don't actually cook the sumac but add it at the very end; doing so preserves the full yet mild flavour of the spice.

Be sure to add the green onions at the last minute as well—if you make this dish ahead of time, add them only after you have reheated the red bell peppers. Serve a dollop of this sauté on top of any meat dish or rice.

Heat oil in a medium pot on medium-high for 1 minute. Add onions and sauté for 5 minutes, or until very slightly golden on the edges. Add bell peppers, salt and brown sugar and cook, stirring regularly, for 1 minute. Stir in sumac, turn off the heat, then add green onions. Serve immediately.

SERVES 6 TO 8

PREP & COOKING TIME
20 minutes

⅓ cup cooking oil

1 lb red, white or yellow onions (2 medium), sliced

3 red bell peppers, seeded and sliced lengthwise in ¼-inch pieces

½ tsp salt

2 Tbsp brown sugar

1 Tbsp + 1 tsp ground sumac

¾ cup finely chopped green onions, white and tender green parts only

SERVE WITH

Pan-seared Breaded Tilapia

Lamb in Creamy Green Cardamom Curry

Fresh Fennel and Pork Curry

VEGETARIAN DISHES

NATY KING OWNS and runs Hazelmere Organic Farm in Surrey, British Columbia. She and her late husband, Gary, started the farm to reintroduce healthy, organic produce to as many people as possible. In their words, "it was never called *organic* when we were kids. It was just fresh produce from the vegetable garden with no pesticides or fertilizers. And it wasn't expensive."

Naty is originally from the Philippines. She told us once, years ago when she was feeding Gary wholesome foods to keep him as comfortable as possible during his cancer treatments, that if there is one thing she has learned, it's that we should mostly eat what our ethnic groups have traditionally eaten for the past hundreds of years. Who—and what—we are physically is based on the genetics of the many generations that went into making us. Just because the foods in the supermarkets have changed doesn't mean our bodies have adapted.

The Indian diet has always been mostly vegetarian, except for the occasional goat-meat or chicken dish. It is debated whether the Hindu god Krishna was vegetarian or if he ate venison when in the forest; the answer lies in mythology, and we can't put a number on how many years ago that could have been. Perhaps because of the lack of meat in our diet, dairy products—milk, yogurt and paneer, a soft mild cheese made from whole milk—hold great importance for Indians. Ghee, which is clarified butter, has always been the choice cooking oil for those who could afford it. All four of our parents grew up eating only foods cooked in ghee, even Meeru's father, who lived in a refugee camp in Delhi for many years after the India-Pakistan partition.

There is no shortage of vegetarian recipes in the Indian repertoire. In fact vegetarianism is what our cuisine is rightly famous for, and nothing can enliven some cabbage or Brussels sprouts like Indian spices. If Indians do eat meat, it is always accompanied by a vegetable and, ideally, a lentil dish. Meals made up solely of meat and potatoes were unheard of until very recently.

We believe that everyone in today's world—whether of Indian heritage or not—needs the vitamins and fibre from vegetables and legumes. There is no better way to enjoy them than to prepare and eat them Indian style.

Curried Devilled Eggs

SERVES 4 TO 6

PREP & COOKING TIME
35 minutes + 30 minutes to chill

¼ cup cooking oil

½ tsp cumin seeds

1 cup chopped (or halved
and thinly sliced)
red onion (1 medium)

1 Tbsp finely chopped
garlic (3 medium cloves)

½ cup finely chopped
tomato (1 medium)

1 tsp salt

1 tsp crushed
cayenne pepper
(optional)

½ tsp ground cumin or
garam masala (page 41)

½ tsp ground fenugreek
seeds (optional)

dash of black pepper

¼ cup plain yogurt
(minimum 2% milk fat), stirred

4 to 5 eggs, hard boiled, cooled
to room temperature and peeled

¼ large jalapeño pepper,
finely chopped

VIKRAM and Meeru both come from egg-loving families, and we have passed on this love of eggs to our own children. We believe that eggs are nutrient rich, and the talk of cholesterol doesn't scare us one bit. We believe that one boiled or poached egg is healthy and quite filling, and we do love our weekend omelets. However, we eat only eggs from organic, cage-free hens because what the hen eats will be in her eggs, and we want our eggs to be as pure as possible.

This recipe was inspired by a feast of boiled eggs with various Ukrainian condiments and white wine at the home of our friends Oleg and Victoria. After that meal Meeru started eating boiled eggs with Ukrainian horseradish for breakfast. It was a healthy, quick meal that filled her up for a few hours. When she ate one of these eggs at a managers' meeting one morning, however, the staff complained that the smell interfered with the aroma of their coffee. We don't recommend these curried eggs for breakfast, either, but they're great as hors d'oeuvres with a glass of white wine or bubbly.

We avoid using the copious amounts of mayonnaise found in traditional devilled eggs—and increase the flavour—by mixing the egg yolks into the masala. Our kitchen staff, who are not fans of mayonnaise, gobbled these up the first time we made them. Now we make them often.

You will most likely have a small amount of the yolk filling left over. It can be refrigerated, covered, for a few days, and it tastes great in a sandwich or with some crackers. Although the jalapeño pepper is a garnish, it adds a bit of heat and a slight acidity; chop the pepper as finely as you can. You won't need very much. The cumin is optional, but it adds to the curry flavour of the dish. Devilled eggs will keep covered and refrigerated for 2 to 3 days.

Heat oil in a small pot on medium-high for 1 minute. Add cumin seeds and allow them to sizzle for 30 seconds, or until the seeds are dark brown but not black. Add onion and sauté for 4 minutes, or until light golden. Add garlic and sauté for another 2 to 3 minutes, or until golden brown. Stir in tomatoes, then immediately add salt, cayenne, ground cumin (or garam masala), fenugreek seeds and black pepper. Sauté the masala for 4 to 5 minutes, or until oil glistens on top. Turn off the heat.

Place yogurt in a small bowl. To prevent curdling, spoon 1 Tbsp of the hot masala into yogurt. Stir well, then pour the yogurt mixture into the masala. Turn on the heat to medium, and mix well but gently. Cook for 3 minutes, stirring continuously, then remove from the heat.

Cut eggs in half lengthwise and carefully scoop the yolks into a medium bowl. Mash yolks with a fork until they are smooth (don't add any water). Add the warm spice masala to yolks and mix well. Using a teaspoon, stuff egg white halves with the filling. Sprinkle ⅛ tsp of the jalapeño pepper over each egg half. Serve immediately, or refrigerate, covered, for 30 minutes, or until chilled.

SERVE WITH

Quinoa Salad with Lentil Sprouts, Celery and Navy Bean Salad, and Baked Jackfruit in Garlic Marinade (as part of a side dish platter)

Yam and Tomato Curry

Quinoa Salad
with Lentil Sprouts

SERVES 8
as a side dish

PREP & COOKING TIME
30 minutes + 15 minutes to cool

1 cup white quinoa

1⅓ cups water

1½ tsp salt

1 Tbsp + 1 tsp olive oil

½ cup finely chopped
green onions

4 oz lentil sprouts (any kind)

⅓ cup finely chopped cilantro

4 oz very finely chopped
celery (2 large ribs)

¼ cup fresh lemon juice

SERVE WITH

Any main dish in this book

At Vij's we came up with a dish made with paneer, cashews, ghee, raw sugar and whipping cream that we now call Punjabi Heart Attack. It is rich and forbiddingly delicious, and it got its name when Meeru and the kitchen staff (all of us Punjabi) joked that we would get a heart attack given how much of it we ate while mastering the recipe. It's impossible to give a recipe for the Heart Attack, since each tablespoon (that is the portion size!) is made à la minute, and we like to keep this recipe whimsical and unwritten.

We didn't feel right serving this rich dish on its own, without a healthy balance, so we came up with this salad. If you imagine yourself sunbathing at the beach in summertime, the hot sun is the Punjabi Heart Attack while the quinoa salad is the cool mist off the ocean that lightly sprinkles your face. At Vij's, our customers finish the quinoa salad just as quickly as they finish the Heart Attack.

You can buy sprouted lentils at many grocers. Some people prefer to eat the lentils crunchy, straight from the box; others prefer to steam the lentils for a few minutes then run them under cold water before serving. Either way will work fine in this recipe. We have read that sprouted lentils are one of the healthiest foods you can treat your body to, but use them quickly, as they last only four to five days.

Place quinoa in a sieve and rinse with cold water for 30 to 45 seconds. (Some packages say to do this for a couple of minutes, but we think that is unnecessary and wastes water.) In a medium pot, combine quinoa, water, ½ tsp of the salt and 1 tsp of the olive oil. (Our water ratio may not match what is written on your quinoa package; feel free to follow those instructions.) Bring to a boil on high heat, then reduce the heat to a simmer, cover and cook for 18 to 20 minutes. Turn off the heat, remove the lid, stir with a fork and cover for 5 minutes. Remove the lid, stir again and set aside to cool to room temperature.

While quinoa is cooking, combine green onions, lentil sprouts, cilantro, celery, lemon juice and the remaining 1 Tbsp of olive oil and 1 tsp of salt. Stir in the cooled quinoa, then cover and refrigerate until you are ready to serve it.

Celery and Navy Bean Salad

For a change of flavour and texture, we serve this cold salad as a side dish with many of our curries. It's a heavier, filling salad, so you don't need to serve that much.

Canned beans don't work in this particular recipe—they are just too soft and mushy. So, before making this recipe, you will need to soak the beans for six hours and then boil them for forty-five minutes, or until they are cooked but still firm. Alternatively, you can cook them in a pressure cooker for thirteen minutes.

In a small frying pan, heat oil on medium-high for 1 minute. Add fennel seeds and allow them to sizzle for 30 seconds. Stir in turmeric and cook for 30 seconds. Turn off the heat and stir in salt and pepper.

In a medium bowl, combine the spice mixture (including the oil) with navy beans, celery and lemon juice. Mix well and serve, either at room temperature or chilled.

SERVES 6
as a side dish

PREP & COOKING TIME
15 minutes + 7 hours to soak and cook the beans + 1 hour to chill

1 Tbsp cooking oil

½ tsp fennel seeds

¼ tsp turmeric

½ tsp salt

¼ tsp black pepper

1 cup raw navy beans, washed, soaked and boiled with ½ tsp salt

3 ribs celery, cut in ¼-inch pieces

1 Tbsp + 1 tsp fresh lemon juice

SERVE WITH

Any main dish in this book

Tangy and Spicy Chopped New Potatoes

SERVES 6
as a side dish

PREP & COOKING TIME
30 minutes

½ cup cooking oil

½ tsp asafoetida (optional)

⅓ to ½ cup puréed
tomato (1 small)

1 tsp salt

1 tsp crushed
cayenne pepper

2 Tbsp ground coriander

2 lbs new potatoes,
unpeeled and cut in
½-inch-wide sticks

1 Tbsp + 1 tsp mango powder

THESE potatoes are like Indian fries and are evocative of the street food that is available all over India. Indians will often eat such snacks around four in the afternoon with a cup of chai or a beer. This recipe may not seem easy to make the first time, but regardless of what the fries look like, they will still taste good. If you don't get the potatoes crispy enough to eat like fries, they're still tangy and delicious as a side dish with dinner or as a funky, satisfying snack—just chop them up and eat them like hash browns on toast. Don't substitute coffee for the chai, as the flavour of the coffee just doesn't match the spices.

In this recipe, we use new potatoes because they remain firm and keep their texture longer than other types, but if you prefer larger fries, feel free to use another variety of potato. We also leave the skin on the potatoes, both for the flavour and for the health benefits. We use tomatoes to absorb the spices and to prevent the potatoes from sticking to the bottom of the pan.

Mango powder is crucial to the tanginess of this dish. And you must use a large pan to cook the potatoes. If the potatoes are overcrowded, they will not cook properly and you will end up with mushy fries. You can also use canned, puréed tomatoes rather than puréeing one small fresh tomato. Finally, you will need a wooden spatula to stir the potatoes; otherwise, they may break while being stirred.

In a large, heavy-bottomed pan with a lid, heat oil on medium-high for 45 seconds. Add asafoetida, stir immediately and continue stirring for 15 seconds. Reduce the heat to medium and carefully stir in tomatoes. Immediately add salt, cayenne and coriander, stir well and sauté for 2 to 3 minutes, or until oil has separated from the tomatoes. Add potatoes and mix well to coat with the spices.

Cook potatoes, uncovered, for 6 to 7 minutes, stirring 2 or 3 times. Check that the spices are not sticking to the bottom of the pan; if they are, reduce the heat slightly. Cover the pan with a lid and cook for 5 minutes. Add mango powder and stir gently but thoroughly. You may notice

that the spices are sticking to the bottom, and that's fine. Cook potatoes, uncovered, for another 3 to 4 minutes, stirring gently and regularly. Poke a potato with a knife to make sure it is cooked; it should be soft but not mushy. Turn off the heat and immediately transfer potatoes to a large serving plate. Using the wooden spatula, scrape any spices stuck to the bottom of the pan, and then spread them over the potatoes.

SERVE WITH

Coconut Vegetable Curry

Mung Beans in Coconut Curry

Stewed Beef and Rapini
in Cumin Curry

Turnips and Tomatoes
in Kalonji Masala

SERVES 6 TO 8

PREP & COOKING TIME
30 minutes

⅓ cup cooking oil

1 tsp kalonji seeds

2 cups puréed
tomatoes (4 medium)

1 Tbsp finely chopped
jalapeño pepper

1½ tsp salt

1 tsp turmeric

1 Tbsp paprika

2 lbs turnips, peeled and
chopped in ½-inch dice

⅓ cup demerara sugar

¾ cup finely chopped cilantro

SERVE WITH

Steamed Sablefish

Coconut Curried Chicken

Grilled Beef Tenderloin with
Almonds and Garlic

IN June 2008 we put crickets (page 136) on our menu. Crickets are low-fat and highly comparable with red meats in terms of protein and iron. As well, they have a minimal carbon footprint. We roasted and ground up the crickets and then added them to buttermilk and whole wheat to make *paranthas* (stuffed flatbreads). We served the cricket paranthas with this turnip recipe.

We knew that seeing crickets on the menu was going to shock and surprise many people, and we thought that adding the word "turnips" to the recipe title would truly kill any chances of anyone ordering the dish. So, we just wrote down "vegetable" instead of turnip and called the crickets, crickets. One of our career highlights was receiving compliments on both the cricket parantha and these turnips. ABC News *Nightline* did a feature story on our dish, as did the CBC's *The National.* Although both the reporters and many of our customers ordered the parantha to taste the crickets, they were nevertheless surprised at how much they enjoyed the turnips. So rid yourself of any memories of boiled turnips, and be sure not to overcook these ones.

You will enjoy this turnip dish with any other type of bread.

Heat oil in a medium pot on medium-high for 1 minute. Add kalonji seeds and allow them to sizzle for 30 seconds. Stir in tomatoes, jalapeño pepper, salt, turmeric and paprika, and sauté for 4 minutes. Stir in turnips, cover, reduce the heat to medium, and cook for 6 to 8 minutes, or until turnips are firm yet cooked. The turnips should be cooked but not soft, as overcooked turnips develop a mushy sweetness. Stir in sugar and cilantro, and serve immediately.

Coconut Curry
for Any Day and Any Dish

Y ou can make this very simple and quick curry and pour it over any meats, seafood or plain vegetables, Indian or non-Indian; steamed, fried or baked. This curry is also great as a dipping sauce for the Spice-encrusted Lamb Popsicles (page 185). Although the concept of this curry isn't very Indian—we don't really dip or pour curry over other foods—it does add either a mild taste to an already spicy dish or a mild Indian flavour to a non-Indian dish. We like it over simple boiled potatoes with skins (Nanaki, Shanik and Vikram) or over salted steamed kale (Meeru).

Place saffron threads in a small bowl. Add water and soak for 30 minutes. Set aside.

In a medium pot, heat oil on medium-high for 45 seconds. Add cumin (or mustard) seeds. Allow cumin seeds to sizzle for 30 seconds (or wait 1 to 2 minutes for mustard seeds to start popping). Sprinkle in asafoetida, stir, then immediately add garlic and sauté for 2 minutes. Add turmeric, salt, cayenne and paprika and sauté for 1 minute.

Stir in coconut milk and stock. Increase the heat to high and bring to a boil. Cover, decrease the heat to low and simmer for 5 minutes. Remove the lid and stir in saffron and its water. Stir in cilantro and serve immediately.

SERVES 6

PREP & COOKING TIME
30 minutes to soak saffron
+ 20 minutes

½ tsp saffron (optional)

¼ cup very hot water (optional)

⅓ cup cooking oil

1 Tbsp cumin seeds or black mustard seeds

½ tsp asafoetida (optional)

2 Tbsp finely chopped garlic (6 medium cloves)

1 tsp turmeric

1½ tsp salt

1 tsp ground cayenne pepper

2 tsp paprika (optional)

5 cups coconut milk

2 cups stock (chicken or vegetable)

½ cup chopped cilantro (optional)

SERVE WITH

Any of the rice pilafs in this book

Any of the steamed fish recipes in this book

Any of the grilled or seared poultry or meat recipes in this book

Ground Fennel Seed Curry

SERVES 6

PREP & COOKING TIME
30 minutes + 25 minutes
to roast and grind fennel seeds

6 Tbsp fennel seeds

⅓ to ½ cup cooking oil

2 cups puréed tomatoes
(4 medium, or canned is
fine, but not crushed)

1 Tbsp salt

1 tsp turmeric

2 Tbsp ground cumin

1 tsp ground fenugreek
seeds (optional)

½ to 1 Tbsp crushed
cayenne pepper

4 cups water

1 cup whipping cream

SERVE WITH

Any white or brown
basmati rice pilaf

Any salted, steamed
or seared fish

FENNEL is a great flavour enhancer for curries made without onions or garlic, so we try to keep one such curry on our menu for Hindus who avoid these foods for religious reasons. This curry is delicious not only with sautéed vegetables but also served over just about any seafood or even duck. You can also use it to make a flavourful bouillabaisse.

If you cook with prawns, just mix them into the curry when you're ready to eat, and heat them on medium for about five minutes, or until they are pink-orange. If you like crispy halibut or trout, you can sear the fish separately in some oil in a frying pan on medium-high heat for three to five minutes per side. If you cook mussels, you can steam them separately and then add them to a bowl of hot fennel seed curry. Finally, this curry is great with Marinated Duck Breast with Mung Bean and Sesame Seed Rice Pilaf (page 175), Steamed Marinated Halibut (page 147) or Steamed Sablefish (page 139).

Heat a 10-inch heavy-bottomed frying pan on high for 1 minute. Add fennel seeds, and, stirring regularly, cook for 2 to 3 minutes, or until slightly darker. Pour roasted seeds onto a plate and allow to cool for 20 minutes. Grind the fennel seeds in a spice (or coffee) grinder. Set aside 2 Tbsp ground fennel seeds for this recipe. Store the remaining seeds in an airtight container in a dark cupboard or drawer for use in other dishes.

In a medium pot, heat oil on medium for 1 minute. Add ground fennel seeds and stir continuously for 30 seconds, or until fennel begins to foam lightly. Carefully and immediately add tomatoes, stirring well. Add salt, turmeric, cumin, fenugreek seeds and cayenne and sauté for 5 minutes, or until oil glistens. If the masala is sticking to the bottom of the pot, add 1 Tbsp more oil.

Pour in water and cream. Stir and bring to a boil. Reduce the heat to low, cover and simmer for 5 minutes. Serve immediately.

Yam and Tomato Curry

SERVES 6

PREP & COOKING TIME
35 minutes

1½ lbs yams (about
2 medium), unpeeled

⅓ cup canola oil

5 Tbsp finely chopped
garlic (15 medium cloves)

4 lightly packed Tbsp
finely chopped ginger

4 cups puréed tomatoes
(8 medium)

1½ tsp turmeric

1 Tbsp ground black mustard
seeds + 2 tsp ground fenugreek
seeds OR 1 Tbsp ground
cumin + 1 Tbsp ground coriander

1 Tbsp crushed
cayenne pepper

1 Tbsp salt

8 cups water

SERVE WITH

Spinach and Split Pea Mash

Black Chickpea Pakoras

Dates and Bitter
Melon Two Ways

WE usually eat this curry as a soup with a big bowl of either white or brown basmati rice. Since cumin and coriander are used so much in Indian food, we prefer to make this dish with ground mustard and fenugreek seeds for a change; remember not to overdo these spices or the curry can become bitter. Cumin and coriander do work well in this curry on their own, or try cumin, coriander and fenugreek seeds together without the mustard seeds. Experiment with all three of these variations depending on your mood and the spices you have on hand.

Cut yams in half and place them in a medium pot. Fill the pot with water until yams are completely submerged, then cover and bring to a boil on high heat. Reduce the heat to medium and continue boiling until yams are soft enough to easily poke with a knife, 20 to 25 minutes. Drain water, and set yams aside to cool for 15 minutes.

Heat oil in a large pot on medium-high for 30 seconds. Add garlic and sauté for 2 minutes, or until golden. Add ginger and sauté for another minute, then carefully add tomatoes and stir. Reduce the heat to medium and stir in turmeric, mustard seeds and fenugreek seeds (or cumin and coriander), cayenne and salt. Stir and sauté masala for 5 minutes, or until oil glistens on top.

Peel yams and discard the skins. Place yams in a medium bowl, and using a potato masher or your fists, mash until smooth. Add water and mashed yams to the masala, stir well and bring to a boil. Reduce the heat to low and simmer for 5 minutes.

Vij's Kitchen Staff's Zucchini Soup

OUR head cook, Amarjeet, asked us to include this recipe in our previous cookbook, but we said no, because we couldn't wrap our heads around the combination of milk and zucchini. For this cookbook, Amarjeet and our entire day staff made the case for including this recipe with a bet that it would be very popular, and when we asked them for it, their faces lit up one by one.

Meeru and Vikram have spent ten years making fun of this recipe, and for ten years, first Vij's and then Rangoli's kitchen staff have been eating this soup once a week. In fact, we had never heard of this recipe before our kitchen staff made it, because it hails from only a certain cluster of villages in the Punjab. When we told our parents about it, they all scoffed at it the way only urbanites can.

As Meeru watched Amarjeet and Sital make this soup, she realized that the kitchen staff prefer their zucchini well cooked and soft, whereas she and Vikram prefer it al dente. It took us ten years to realize that if we cooked the zucchini less, we would have loved this soup and included it in our previous cookbook. As we write, it is late September, and Stephen Gallagher, our CSA (page 94) farmer, is sending us gigantic zucchini. Amarjeet is very happy. In the winter, when carrots are sweet, tender and in season in the Punjab, it is made with carrots instead of zucchini. We haven't made the leap to carrots, but if you like cooked carrots, use the same quantity of carrots as you would zucchini. Serve this soup with rice or bread for a warm, light meal.

In a medium pot, heat oil on medium-high for 1 minute. Add cumin seeds and allow them to sizzle for 30 to 45 seconds, or until they darken. Stir in onion and sauté for 10 minutes, or until quite browned but not burned. Add garlic and sauté for 1 to 2 minutes, or until golden, then stir in ginger, jalapeño pepper, garam masala, salt and turmeric. Sauté spices for 3 to 4 minutes, stirring regularly, then add zucchini and water and stir well. Cook zucchini for 3 to 4 minutes, or until it is almost cooked to the texture you prefer. Add milk, stir and bring to a light boil. As soon as the milk begins to boil lightly, turn off the heat. Stir in cilantro.

SERVES 4 TO 6

PREP & COOKING TIME
30 to 40 minutes

⅓ cup cooking oil

1 Tbsp cumin seeds

2 cups finely chopped onion (1 large)

2 Tbsp finely chopped garlic (6 medium cloves)

2 Tbsp finely chopped ginger

1 Tbsp chopped jalapeño pepper

1½ tsp garam masala (page 41)

1 Tbsp salt

1 tsp turmeric

2 lbs zucchini, cut in ½-inch dice

½ cup water

2½ cups whole milk

½ cup chopped cilantro (or more, to taste)

SERVE WITH

Serve this dish on its own.

Baked Jackfruit
in Garlic Marinade

SERVES 6
as a side dish

PREP & COOKING TIME
35 minutes + 25 minutes to
roast and grind fennel seeds

6 Tbsp fennel seeds or
1 Tbsp garam masala (page 41)

two 18-oz cans jackfruit, drained

⅓ cup cooking oil

1 tsp paprika

½ tsp ground cayenne pepper

1 Tbsp + 1 tsp finely chopped
garlic (4 medium cloves)

½ tsp salt

THE spice combinations in this recipe are very similar to many other Indian dishes, but they taste completely different when used with jackfruit. You can use either garam masala or ground fennel seeds, but don't use these spices together. This recipe is for a side dish or an appetizer, as it is surprisingly strong in taste. Two to three pieces per person is enough. It is meant to be eaten with a knife and fork, which is rare with Indian food; advise people to cut the fruit along its threads.

Jackfruit is an Asian-grown fruit that is ripened and used in desserts in Thailand and the Philippines. In India, we use raw, green jackfruit in savoury dishes. It grows wild like coconuts in southern India, and it is like artichoke hearts in flavour and texture. Given jackfruit's texture, coming up with great recipes for it isn't all that easy, but when we do, we get quite excited. It is a very popular ingredient in Indian cuisine, and we find that virtually all of our customers enjoy it.

In North America, only canned jackfruit is available on a regular basis. We have cooked with fresh jackfruit as well, but it's quite the effort to peel and cut it, so we suggest you use the canned variety. Since most canned jackfruit has added salt, you don't need much in the recipe. Also, the weights of canned jackfruit will vary slightly, but you should have six to eight pieces in a can. We recommend that you cook the jackfruit on a baking sheet lined with aluminum foil to minimize the mess; however, placing it directly on the baking sheet will result in jackfruit with a crispier outside.

If using fennel seeds, heat a 10-inch heavy-bottomed frying pan on high for 1 minute. Add fennel seeds, and, stirring regularly, cook for 2 to 3 minutes, or until slightly darker. Pour roasted seeds onto a plate and allow to cool for 20 minutes. Grind the fennel seeds in a spice (or coffee) grinder. Set aside 1 tsp of the ground fennel seeds for this recipe and store the rest in an airtight container in a dark cupboard or drawer for use in other dishes.

Place jackfruit pieces in a tea towel and gently rub each one to dry it. Transfer jackfruit pieces to a bowl.

Preheat the oven to 450°F. Line a baking sheet with aluminum foil.

In a large bowl, combine oil, fennel (or garam masala), paprika, cayenne, garlic and salt. Add jackfruit pieces and mix well to coat completely

with the spices and oil. Spread jackfruit on the baking sheet. Spoon any leftover spices from the bowl over jackfruit. The mixing bowl should be fairly empty of any spices. Bake on the middle rack for 15 minutes. Jackfruit should be sizzling and have a nice gloss from the oil (if jackfruit is directly on the baking sheet, there will be some light charring on the pieces). One sign that jackfruit is cooked is that some threads of jackfruit will have separated and are sticking out. If no threads are visible and jackfruit hasn't charred, bake for another 5 minutes. Threads or no threads, remove jackfruit from the oven.

SERVE WITH

Any seafood dish

Chicken with Crimini Mushrooms and Saffron Curry

Marinated Duck Breast with Mung Bean and Sesame Seed Rice Pilaf

Spicy Cauliflower "Steak"

MEERU loves to tease Vikram about two things: how much he loves meat and, after his years of studying in Europe, how she could never be as mannered and proper at a dining table as he is. One evening, when she was in charge of the meal, she made this vegetarian steak as a replacement for his regular meat steak. She wanted to feed him vegetables but (half-jokingly) give him the pleasure of using a fork and steak knife in a proper dining-table setting.

Like eggplant, cauliflower is a staple vegetable throughout India. Its taste and texture are a perfect match for Indian spices. You will rarely meet an Indian who doesn't enjoy cauliflower, and we grew up eating it once a week.

You could just as easily cut up the cauliflower into smaller florets in this recipe, but we enjoy the "steak" cut and also find it's easier to reheat this thicker cut the next day. Although there's no sauce here, it's still great with rice. And if you want some meat on the side, the Ground Lamb, Beef and Lentil Kebobs (page 186) are perfect.

This cauliflower steak eventually ended up on our Rangoli menu.

Cut cauliflower, as you would a pie, into 6 pieces if it's a smaller head and 8 pieces if it's a larger one. Wash and carefully place large cauliflower pieces in a colander to drain.

Combine oil and tomatoes in a large wide pot on medium-high heat. (Since the pot is large, you may need to turn it on to high if your stove burner is small.) Add ginger, salt, turmeric, cumin, coriander, cayenne, cloves and cinnamon, stir well and sauté for 3 to 4 minutes, or until oil glistens from tomatoes.

Reduce the heat to low while you mix in cauliflower. Carefully place each large piece of cauliflower into the pot and gently stir so that the tomato masala covers all the pieces. If necessary, use a large spoon to ladle tomato masala into the nooks and crannies of the cauliflower pieces.

Increase the heat to medium, cover and cook for 8 to 10 minutes, stirring once halfway through. When you stir, if you notice that the cauliflower isn't cooking, increase the heat. If it's sticking to the bottom of the pot, decrease the heat. Pierce one of the larger pieces with a knife to see if it is soft (not mushy). If necessary, cook cauliflower, covered, for another 1 to 2 minutes. (If florets have broken apart because they overcooked, don't worry; this dish is still delicious.)

SERVES 6 TO 8
depending on the size
of the cauliflower

PREP & COOKING TIME
30 minutes

1 head cauliflower,
outside stalks cut off

½ cup cooking oil

1½ cups puréed or
crushed canned tomatoes

1 Tbsp finely chopped ginger

1½ tsp salt

1 tsp turmeric

1 Tbsp ground cumin

1 Tbsp ground coriander

1 tsp ground cayenne pepper

10 cloves (optional)

3-inch cinnamon stick (optional)

SERVE WITH

Spicy Peas and Mashed
Potato Toasted Sandwiches

Punjabi Lentil Curry OR
Mung Beans in Coconut Curry

Oven-baked Chicken
and Potatoes in Yogurt and
Date Curry

Green Beans, Potatoes and Spinach
in Coconut Curry

SERVES 6

PREP & COOKING TIME
40 minutes

⅓ cup cooking oil

2 ½ cups puréed tomatoes
(5 medium, or canned is fine)

1½ tsp salt

1 tsp turmeric

1 Tbsp ground black
mustard seeds

1 Tbsp crushed cayenne
pepper (optional)

1 cup water

1 lb potatoes, unpeeled
and cut in ½-inch cubes

½ lb green beans, trimmed
and cut in 1-inch pieces

1½ cups coconut milk, stirred

½ lb fresh spinach with stems
(1 bunch), washed and chopped

SERVE WITH

Indian-style Tomato,
Onion and Paneer Bruschetta

Eggplant and Paneer Pâté

Mango Reduction
Curry with Prawns

Marinated Duck Breast with
Mung Bean and Sesame Rice
Pilaf (without the duck)

ALTHOUGH we've estimated forty minutes of preparation and cooking time for this curry, if you're versed at chopping, this is a very quick main dish. Like most cooks we've developed certain themes over the years that we tend to repeat because we just like them so much. This dish features one such theme: tomatoes, mustard seeds and coconut milk. You can use just about any combination of vegetables and ingredients to make this recipe. At various times, we have added cubes of paneer (page 52) or deep-fried jackfruit instead of potatoes.

This rich and filling dish is meant to be a feature vegetarian dish rather than a side vegetarian dish. Serve it with rice or any type of bread.

Place oil and tomatoes in a medium pot on medium-high heat and cook for 1 minute. Add salt, turmeric, mustard seeds and cayenne, stir and sauté for 3 to 4 minutes or until oil glistens in the bubbles of the boiling tomatoes. Stir in water and potatoes and bring to a boil. Reduce the heat to low, cover and cook for 10 minutes. Remove the lid and stir in green beans. Cover and cook an additional 5 to 8 minutes, or until potatoes are cooked through.

Stir in coconut milk and increase the heat to medium. Bring to a boil, then stir in spinach, cover and reduce the heat to low. Cook for 1 minute, or until spinach wilts into the curry. Serve immediately.

Red Bell Pepper
and Shallot Curry

At Vij's, we serve this dish as a vegetable accompaniment to our Chicken Breast and Thighs in Clove, Black Cardamom and Yogurt Curry (page 172), as it goes well with the stronger spices in the chicken. It's a quick, simple recipe that is actually delicious on its own served with rice, chapatti or a baguette. Although it is not heavily spiced, this dish does have some heat, so adjust the quantity of jalapeño pepper to your tolerance.

Separate the white part of the green onions from the green part. Place them in two separate bowls.

Heat oil in a heavy, medium pot on medium-high for 30 seconds. Add cumin seeds and allow them to sizzle for 30 to 45 seconds, or until they become a darker brown. Immediately add shallots and white parts of the green onions and sauté for 7 to 8 minutes, or until golden. Add tomatoes, jalapeño peppers, salt, turmeric, paprika and mustard seeds. Reduce the heat to medium and cook this masala for 10 minutes, or until oil separates and glistens on top.

Stir in bell peppers and cook, covered, for 3 to 5 minutes, or until they reach your preferred texture. Stir in green parts of the green onions and serve immediately.

SERVES 6 TO 8
as a side dish

PREP & COOKING TIME
45 minutes

1 bunch green onions, white and green parts, chopped in thin rounds

½ cup cooking oil

1 Tbsp cumin seeds

2 cups (11 oz) thinly sliced shallots

1 lb tomatoes (3 large), chopped

3 large jalapeño peppers, finely chopped

1 Tbsp salt

1 tsp turmeric

1 tsp paprika

1 tsp ground black mustard seeds

3 to 4 red bell peppers, seeded and chopped lengthwise in ½-inch slices

SERVE WITH

Mushroom Medley in Potato Curry

Sautéed Spinach and Tomatoes with Paneer

Chickpea and Cucumber Curry

Chicken Breast and Thighs in Clove, Black Cardamom and Yogurt Curry

87

Oven-baked Spicy Brussels Sprouts Crumble
and Sour Cream Curry

SERVES 6

PREP & COOKING TIME
45 minutes (while the
Brussels sprouts bake,
start cooking the curry)

Baked Brussels sprouts

1½ lbs Brussels sprouts,
cut in ½-inch dice

2 Tbsp ground cumin

½ Tbsp salt

½ tsp crushed cayenne
pepper (optional)

2 tsp mango powder

1 Tbsp cooking oil

Sour cream curry

½ cup sour cream

½ cup buttermilk

⅓ cup cooking oil

1 cup chopped onion (1 medium)

2 Tbsp finely chopped
garlic (6 medium cloves)

2 cups puréed tomatoes
(4 medium, or canned is fine,
but not crushed)

2 Tbsp ground yellow
mustard seeds (optional)

1 tsp ground cayenne
pepper (optional)

2 tsp salt

1½ Tbsp garam masala
(page 41) or ground cumin

1 tsp ground fenugreek
seeds (optional)

3½ cups water

Meeru loves Brussels sprouts, unless they are overcooked and, therefore, bitter. She tries to squeeze them onto the menu at every party and has even managed to serve them as hors d'oeuvres. This recipe sounds even more bizarre, as it's her alternative to eggs Benedict: sour cream curry takes the place of hollandaise sauce and finely chopped Brussels sprouts stand in for the eggs!

Serve this vegetarian dish at an Indian brunch or for an early supper—just don't serve it too early in the morning, since the spices may be a bit much for some people's stomachs. This crumble is very satisfying served on whichever bread you prefer (though we don't recommend Russian-style rye breads because they don't match the spices). It is also very tasty over plain basmati rice.

Watch the cooking time carefully, as ovens vary in temperature. Ours is a commercial oven, so unless yours is also a heavy-duty oven, you may need to heat the Brussels sprouts for a minute or two longer. Remember that the crumble may also take a bit longer if you keep opening the oven door to check on it. Also, if you don't have buttermilk, use a total of one cup of sour cream; it will be a richer curry but just as good. If you purée canned whole tomatoes, be sure to include all their water.

Baked Brussels sprouts Preheat the oven to 400°F. On a large baking tray, toss Brussels sprouts with cumin, salt, cayenne, mango powder and oil. Bake for 15 minutes, carefully stirring them once after 6 minutes. (The spices should be cooked and the Brussels sprouts slightly dry but not wilted.) Remove from the oven and set aside.

Sour cream curry In a medium bowl, combine sour cream and buttermilk. Set aside.

Heat oil in a medium pot on medium-high for 45 seconds. Add onion and sauté for 5 minutes, or until golden brown. Add garlic and sauté for 2 to 3 minutes, or until garlic is also golden brown. Stir in tomatoes, mustard seeds, cayenne, salt, garam masala (or cumin) and fenugreek seeds and sauté for 5 minutes, or until oil glistens on top. Stir in water and bring to a boil. Reduce the heat to low and simmer for 5 minutes.

To prevent curdling, spoon about 3 Tbsp of the hot curry into the sour cream–buttermilk mixture. Stir well, then pour the sour cream–buttermilk mixture into the pot of curry. Using a whisk, mix well and simmer, stirring continuously, for 5 minutes, or until the curry reaches a gentle boil. Remove from the heat.

Top baked Brussels sprouts with sour cream curry and serve immediately.

SERVE WITH

Serve this dish with bread or on top of a 2-inch cube of paneer per serving.

89

Spicy Peas and Mashed Potato Toasted Sandwiches

MAKES 10 SANDWICHES

PREP & COOKING TIME
45 minutes (if you've already
made the sour cream dressing)

1 lb potatoes,
peeled or unpeeled

10 oz frozen peas

⅓ cup cooking oil

1 medium onion,
finely chopped

1 Tbsp finely chopped ginger

1½ tsp salt

1 Tbsp garam masala
(page 41) or ground cumin

1 Tbsp crushed cayenne pepper

½ cup finely chopped
cilantro (optional)

10 ciabatta rolls or 20 slices of
bread or 2 to 3 sliced baguettes

1 cup sour cream
Indian dressing (page 43)

½ English cucumber, sliced
in thin rounds (optional)

WHEN we get tired of eating curries, we make these sandwiches for kitchen staff lunch at the restaurants and use our sour cream Indian dressing (page 43) in place of mayonnaise or Thousand Island dressing. This is our own variation on a samosa.

The only time-consuming aspect of this recipe is boiling the potatoes (very easy) and mashing them once they've cooled off a bit. It's better to buy a few smaller potatoes to boil rather than one large one, which would take longer. Once the peas and potatoes are cooked, just spread them onto any toasted bread—ciabatta, regular sliced bread, baguette, etc.

Feel free to add more onions and ginger to this recipe, if you wish. We've made these sandwiches many times, with many different amounts of onions and ginger, and they are always delicious. Be sure to use frozen peas instead of fresh, blanched ones, as you need the soft texture. Any extra filling will keep refrigerated in an airtight container for up to a week.

Place potatoes in a pot, cover with water and bring to a boil on high heat. Reduce the heat to medium, cover and boil for 30 minutes, or until soft but not mushy when pierced with a knife. (The boiling time will vary greatly depending on the size of your potatoes.) Drain potatoes and set aside to cool.

While potatoes are boiling, place frozen peas in a colander, rinse them in cold water (this quickens the thawing) and allow them to thaw over the sink.

Once potatoes have cooled, transfer them to a medium bowl and mash with a potato masher. (Do not add any of the potato cooking water or milk or butter when you mash the potatoes.)

In a medium pot, heat oil on high for 45 seconds, add onion and sauté for 7 to 8 minutes, or until browned. Reduce the heat to medium, stir in ginger and sauté for 30 seconds. Add salt, garam masala (or cumin) and cayenne and sauté for 1 minute. Add peas and potatoes and stir well, cooking for 3 to 4 minutes, or until vegetables are hot. Mix in cilantro.

Lightly toast the bread and spread with the sour cream dressing. Arrange the bread slices dressing-side up, and divide the pea-potato mixture equally among ten of them. Spread the mixture evenly across the dressing, then top each sandwich with slices of cucumber. Place the second slice of bread on top of each sandwich and serve immediately.

SERVE WITH

Spicy Cauliflower "Steak"

Indian-style Tomato, Onion and Paneer Bruschetta (as part of an appetizer platter; cut the sandwiches into bite-sized pieces)

Serve this dish on its own.

Yogurt Curry

35 minutes (or 45 minutes if you add chopped vegetables)

4 cups plain yogurt (minimum 2% milk fat), stirred

½ cup chickpea flour

5 cups water

⅓ cup cooking oil

1 Tbsp cumin seeds

2 cups chopped onion (1 large)

2 Tbsp chopped garlic (6 medium cloves) (optional)

2 Tbsp chopped ginger (optional)

1 tsp turmeric

1 Tbsp salt

2 tsp ground coriander (optional)

1 Tbsp crushed cayenne pepper (optional)

1 tsp ground fenugreek seeds (optional)

15 fresh curry leaves (optional)

5 oz green beans, trimmed and cut in ¼-inch pieces (optional)

1 cup frozen peas (optional)

½ cup chopped cilantro or 1 Tbsp dried green fenugreek leaves (optional)

PUNJABIS—HINDU or Sikh—simply call this dish "curry"; whenever we say just "curry," it means this yogurt dish. This curry is a traditional Punjabi dish that we either love like crazy or just wish didn't exist. According to our informal survey, about 80 per cent of us love it and 20 per cent can easily live without it. Meeru grew up eating curry mostly for lunch in the summertime while her father was at work because he's one of the 20 per cent that can't stand it. The staff at Vij's make curry every Sunday because our head cook, Amarjeet, doesn't like it and does not work on Sundays. Ironically, Amarjeet also makes curry for lunch every Sunday because her own family loves it!

If we are making curry for ourselves or other adults, we use all of the spices listed below. If we are making this dish for Nanaki and Shanik, we use only the few spices that aren't optional. The Vij-Dhalwala family loves curry and eats it for lunch or dinner two to three times a month. The best curry is made from a slightly sour yogurt, so it is perfect for using up yogurt that has been sitting in your fridge for a while but hasn't yet gone bad.

Although we eat plain curry at home, you can add various ingredients, such as green beans or peas, or, as we do at Rangoli, you can even serve it over seared white fish such as tilapia (page 145). Adding fish to this traditionally vegetarian dish was a shock for many of the kitchen staff, and Vikram and Meeru didn't tell their parents for fear of the comments. The Black Chickpea Pakoras (page 124) are also delicious in this curry. If you make this recipe exactly as it is described here, you will have a tangy-spicy, rich yogurt curry; however, mix and match the spices to suit your own preferences or to use what you have in the cupboard.

The one thing all Punjabis agree on is that this curry is eaten with white basmati rice. Serve it with salted, diced cucumbers on the side.

In a large bowl, whisk together yogurt, chickpea flour and water until smooth. Set aside.

Heat oil on medium-high for 45 seconds. Add cumin seeds and allow them sizzle for 45 seconds, or until they darken. Immediately stir in onion and sauté for 6 to 8 minutes, or until golden brown for a milder

flavour or slightly darker brown for a toastier flavour. Stir in garlic and
sauté for 1 minute, then add ginger and sauté for 30 seconds.

Add turmeric, salt, coriander, cayenne and fenugreek seeds, then stir
well and sauté for 1 minute. Stir in yogurt–chickpea flour–water mixture,
whisking well to break up any clumps. Bring to a boil, add curry leaves
and reduce the heat to medium and cook for 20 minutes, stirring occasionally. If you are using green beans and/or peas, add them in the last
5 minutes of cooking. In the final seconds of cooking, add cilantro (or
fenugreek leaves), stir well, remove from the heat and serve immediately.

SERVE WITH

Serve this dish on its own.

Coconut Vegetable Curry

SERVES 6 TO 8

PREP & COOKING TIME
40 minutes

⅓ cup cooking oil

½ tsp asafoetida

2 cups puréed tomatoes
(4 medium)

1 Tbsp salt

1 Tbsp ground
cumin (optional)

1 tsp ground
coriander (optional)

1 Tbsp crushed
cayenne pepper

½ Tbsp turmeric

1 cup water

2 lbs celery root, peeled
and cut in 1-inch dice

1 large cauliflower (about 2 lbs),
cut into medium florets

1 cup coconut milk

7 oz rapini (without the
tough bottom stems),
cut in ½-inch lengths

THE night that our friends Jeremy and Heather came over to make kebobs (page 186), they brought over a big plastic bin full of Brussels sprouts and beets instead of wine or flowers. Jeremy and Heather belong to a CSA (community-supported agriculture) farm and receive a weekly twenty-pound bin full of local, organic vegetables from the farm. They had been doing well finding recipes for all the new vegetables they were cooking with, but they were stumped by the Brussels sprouts. Jeremy was hoping to learn some Indian beet recipes as well.

When we looked into the bin, we could immediately see that these Brussels sprouts were incredibly fresh—they were still on their stalks and were full of their farm dirt. The beets were bright purple, and their flavour was incredible. The following spring Vij's restaurant joined Nathan Creek Organic Farm to support our local CSA. For about twenty weeks during the summer growing season, we receive three twenty-pound bins of vegetables a week. (CSA exists throughout North America, but each farm—even those in the same area—grows its own mix of fruits and vegetables.) For the restaurant, we also buy produce from other non-CSA local farms so that we have as much variety of vegetables as possible.

Purchasing a share in a CSA farm, which entitles you to a weekly bin of produce, is a good, affordable way to support local agriculture and to commit yourself to cooking and eating organic, local produce without having to do the shopping. If, during busy weeks, you get overwhelmed by the amount of produce, share it with your neighbours just as you would any extra veggies you grow on your balcony or in your backyard.

We came up with this recipe specifically to use with the surprise vegetables in our CSA bins. We also make this at home, specifically for Nanaki, and without the cumin, since she prefers mild curries and loves coconut milk. You can use just about any seasonal vegetable—adjust your cooking time accordingly—as the velvety coconut and light spicing are a perfect background for all vegetable combinations, including Brussels sprouts. Be sure to peel the celery root's thick skin, and don't worry that it weighs much less once that has been done. As well, when preparing the rapini (also known as Italian broccoli), chop off the bottom two to three inches of the tough stems.

Serve this hearty curry in big bowls over rice.

In a large pan, heat oil on medium-high for 45 seconds. Sprinkle in asa-foetida and allow it to sizzle for 30 seconds. Carefully add tomatoes, then stir and add salt, cumin, coriander, cayenne and turmeric. Sauté for 5 minutes, or until oil glistens on top.

Add water, stir and bring to a boil. Reduce the heat to medium, stir in celery root, cover and cook for 5 minutes. Stir in cauliflower, cover and cook for 5 more minutes. Pour in coconut milk, then bring back to a boil and stir in rapini. Cook for 1 to 2 minutes, while stirring, then turn off the heat.

SERVE WITH

Steamed Sablefish OR
Steamed Marinated Halibut

Dungeness Crab Spoons
with Coconut, Cilantro and
Jalapeño Peppers

Spice-encrusted Lamb Popsicles

Mushroom Medley
in Potato Curry

THIS dish is an Indian soup that is eaten like a potato chowder, and because it is made with buttermilk, you get a good serving of calcium. Boil the potatoes and have them peeled and roughly mashed before you start making the curry, and chop the mushrooms so that the various varieties cook at the same time. We use a medley of shiitake, oyster and crimini mushrooms, but use whichever ones you prefer. Make sure you have a ladle and a whisk on hand for this recipe.

Place potatoes in a large pot, cover with water and bring to a boil on high heat. Cover, reduce the heat to medium and boil for 45 minutes, or until potatoes are soft but not mushy when pierced with a knife. Drain potatoes and set aside to cool.

Once potatoes are cool, use your fingers or a sharp knife to peel off and discard the skins. Roughly mash the potatoes using your fists or a potato masher. (Be sure to leave the potatoes a bit chunky, as you want some texture in the soup.)

In a large heavy-bottomed pot, heat oil on medium-high for 45 seconds. Add cumin seeds and allow them to sizzle for 30 seconds. Add garlic and sauté for 1 to 2 minutes, or until golden. Stir in ginger and sauté for 30 seconds, then add salt, coriander, cayenne and turmeric, and sauté for 1 minute. Reduce the heat to low, stir in potatoes and mix well. Increase the heat to medium-high, add the 5 cups of water and stir thoroughly. Bring to a boil and reduce the heat to low.

Pour buttermilk into a large bowl (or the same one in which you kept the potatoes). To prevent the buttermilk from separating in the soup, use a ladle to spoon about 1½ cups of the hot potato curry into the buttermilk. Whisk the mixture until it is well combined. Carefully spoon all of the buttermilk into the pot of curry. Using the whisk, mix well and, stirring continuously, bring to a boil on low heat. Add mushrooms and cook for about 2 minutes, or until slightly wilted. Remove from the heat and serve immediately.

SERVES 6

PREP & COOKING TIME
45 minutes + 45 minutes to boil potatoes

1½ lbs potatoes, unpeeled

½ cup cooking oil

1 Tbsp cumin seeds

3 Tbsp finely chopped garlic (9 medium cloves)

3 Tbsp finely chopped ginger

1 Tbsp salt

2½ Tbsp ground coriander

1 Tbsp crushed cayenne pepper

1 tsp turmeric

5 cups water

2½ cups buttermilk

6 oz mushrooms, chopped

SERVE WITH

Brown Basmati Rice

Spicy Cauliflower "Steak"

Spicy Pulled Pork Roast with Garlic

Portobello Mushrooms
and Red Bell Peppers and Creamy Curry

SERVES 6

PREP & COOKING TIME
40 to 50 minutes (if you have already made the paneer)

Creamy curry

4 cups whipping cream

2 ½ Tbsp fresh lemon juice

¼ cup cooking oil

2 ½ Tbsp finely chopped garlic (7 or 8 medium cloves) or 1 medium onion, finely chopped

1 tsp turmeric

1 ½ tsp salt

1 Tbsp paprika

½ tsp ground cayenne pepper

Grilled mushrooms and peppers

⅓ cup cooking oil

1 large red onion, thinly sliced

1 Tbsp ground cumin

1 tsp salt

6 large portobello mushrooms, cut in ½-inch-thick slices

3 red bell peppers, halved lengthwise, seeded and cut in ½-inch slices

12 slices of paneer (page 52) or toasted baguette, each ¼-inch thick

THIS is the most popular vegetarian dish at Rangoli, and we have had it on our menu there since Day 1. We change all the menu items except for this one. We serve this curry on a slice of homemade paneer (page 52), which makes a very rich appetizer. You can buy paneer at most Indian grocers. If you don't have any or you don't have the time to make it, serve the curry over toasted baguette or even some steamed spinach or boiled, salted potatoes. Unfortunately, other cheeses are not good substitutes in this dish.

We buy organic mushrooms and don't wash them—we just wipe them carefully and thoroughly. Washing and drying your portobello mushrooms is fine too. We use one portobello mushroom and half a bell pepper per person. If you prefer more or less, you can easily adjust the quantities in this recipe accordingly. We prefer to choose the flavour of either garlic or onion, as the two combined get a bit muddled in so much cream.

Creamy curry Combine cream and lemon juice in a large bowl and set aside.

Heat oil in a medium pan on medium for 1 minute. Add garlic (or onion) and sauté, stirring regularly, for 3 to 4 minutes for garlic (or 6 or 8 minutes for onion), or until golden brown. Be sure to scrape garlic from the sides of the pan if it starts to stick. Add turmeric, salt, paprika and cayenne and stir well. Sauté spices for 2 to 3 minutes, then turn off the heat.

Mix the garlic- (or onion)-spice mixture into the cream. Pour some of the cream back into the pan, swirling it a bit to ensure you remove any garlic or spices stuck on the sides. Pour the cream mixture back into the bowl. Set aside. This sauce will keep refrigerated, covered, for 2 days (check the expiry date on your whipping cream, too) so you can make it ahead and reheat.

Grilled mushrooms and peppers In a large frying pan, heat oil for 45 seconds on medium-high. Add onion and sauté for 5 minutes, or until edges are brown. Stir in cumin and salt and sauté for 1 minute. Add mushrooms and bell peppers and sauté for 3 minutes, stirring regularly. Turn off the heat and allow to cool for 5 minutes.

Stir in the garlic (or onion) cream mixture. Turn the heat on to medium-low and bring to a boil, stirring continuously. The mushrooms and bell peppers should be ready to eat, but if you prefer your vegetables on the softer side, heat them for another minute.

Arrange two slices of paneer (or baguette) on each plate. Divide vegetables and cream curry equally overtop. The hot curry will warm the paneer (or baguette). Serve immediately.

SERVE WITH
Serve this dish on its own.

Rapini and Shiitake Mushroom Curry

SERVES 6

PREP & COOKING TIME
30 minutes

½ cup cooking oil

¼ to ½ cup all-purpose flour

2 cups crushed tomatoes
(canned work best)

1½ tsp salt

1 tsp turmeric

1 tsp ground cayenne pepper

3 Tbsp ground panch poran
or 1 Tbsp ground cumin or
garam masala (page 41)

1 cup plain yogurt
(minimum 2% milk fat)
whisked with 5 cups water

6 oz rapini (without the tough
bottom stems), finely chopped

6 oz mushrooms, roughly
broken up or thinly sliced

SERVE WITH

Marinated Duck Breast with
Mung Bean and Sesame Seed
Rice Pilaf (in place of the curry)

Grilled Beef Tenderloin
with Almonds and Garlic

Any non-Indian grilled
or seared meat dish

THIS fall curry is very versatile and forgiving. It also goes well with grilled or seared meats such as beef, pork or lamb tenderloin or chops, or oven-roasted chicken. As with any vegetarian curry, you can also enjoy this dish on its own with a bowl of rice. You can add anywhere from ¼ to ½ cup flour, depending on how thick you prefer your sauce. To make it a soup, just add an extra cup of water to the recipe.

Use any green leafy vegetable if you can't find rapini. Once we even sautéed broccoli separately in some oil and added it at the very end. If you use fresh spinach, you don't need to chop it finely, as it cooks very quickly and will be absorbed into the curry.

In this recipe we prefer shiitake, oyster and chanterelle mushrooms—all of them either roughly broken up or cut in small pieces. If you use firmer button, crimini or portobello mushrooms, be sure to cut them in thin slices.

If you don't have any panch poran, use ground cumin or garam masala (page 41) instead. Although these spices will change the original flavour of the curry, it will not taste bad—just different. The one ingredient you must use in the curry is the yogurt. It adds a mild tang that goes very well with the greens and mushrooms. Be sure to use a yogurt with some fat in it, as the no-fat varieties do not have a rich enough flavour.

In a large pot, heat oil on medium-high for 45 seconds. Add flour and reduce the heat to medium. Cook, stirring regularly, for 5 minutes, or until flour is light gold. Keeping your head away from the pot, gently pour in tomatoes and stir. Add salt, turmeric, cayenne and panch poran (or cumin or garam masala) and sauté for 4 minutes, stirring regularly. The mixture will be a bit doughy, so stirring will keep it from sticking to the bottom of the pot.

Add the yogurt-water mixture. Using a whisk, stir well to break up any clumps of flour. Bring to a boil, then reduce the heat to low and simmer, uncovered, for 10 minutes. Add the rapini and mushrooms, stir and cook for 1 minute. Turn off the heat and serve.

Brown Basmati
and Portobello Mushroom Pilaf

SERVES 8

PREP & COOKING TIME
45 minutes to 1 hour (including
the time to cook the brown rice)

Rice

2 cups brown basmati rice

2 to 3 Tbsp butter or cooking oil

1 large onion, finely chopped

4 cups water or stock
(chicken or vegetable)

1 tsp salt

Mushrooms

2 to 3 Tbsp cooking oil

1 Tbsp cumin seeds

1 Tbsp finely chopped
garlic (3 medium cloves)

½ medium tomato, chopped

1 tsp salt

1 tsp black pepper or ground
cayenne pepper (optional)

1 tsp dried green
fenugreek leaves

10 oz mushrooms,
cut in 1-inch slices

SERVE WITH

Coconut Vegetable Curry

Stewed Beef and
Rapini in Cumin Curry

Fresh Fennel and Pork Curry

ALTHOUGH you can use any type of mushroom in this pilaf, we prefer portobello mushrooms for their firm texture. Shiitakes go very limp if you overcook them, and we don't think their soft texture matches the firmness of the brown rice. The same goes for oyster mushrooms if you overcook them. Criminis (brown button mushrooms) and white button mushrooms hold their shape well, but their flavours aren't as strong as portobellos. We use a small amount of chopped tomato so that we can use less oil yet not burn the spices while they're sautéing. The garlic in the mushrooms tastes great with the onions in the brown rice.

Serve this pilaf on its own as a main dish with side pickles or chutneys, or serve it as a side dish and refrigerate any leftover pilaf for the next day's lunch or dinner. Add a bit of water to the pot when you reheat this pilaf.

Rice See method on page 55, and be sure to include the onions in the recipe. Prepare the mushroom mixture while the rice is cooking.

Mushrooms In a medium frying pan, heat oil on medium-high for 45 seconds. Sprinkle in cumin seeds and allow them to sizzle for 15 to 30 seconds, or until dark brown. Add garlic and sauté for 2 minutes, or until golden brown. Stir in tomato. Add salt, black pepper (or cayenne) and fenugreek leaves, stir well and sauté for 1 minute. Add mushrooms and stir well. Reduce the heat to medium and continue cooking for 4 minutes, or until mushrooms release water. (When you first add the mushrooms and stir, the masala may stick to the pan and it will look messy. This will all change when they release water.) As soon as mushrooms become slightly wilted, turn off the heat so that you don't overcook them. Set aside until the rice is cooked.

Pour mushrooms into cooked rice. Spoon a quarter cup of rice into the frying pan and stir it around to soak up all the garlic and spices. Pour this rice back into the rest of the mushroom-rice mixture and stir well to combine.

Mushroom and Celery Root
Basmati Rice Pilaf

CELERY root has a gentle, mild celery flavour and a firm beet-like texture. This recipe calls for a pound and a half of celery root, but its skin is quite thick, so you will end up with much less (about eleven ounces) once you've peeled it. You may have to use a knife instead of a vegetable peeler to do this.

Mushrooms and celery root go together very nicely, but you can also use green or red bell peppers, green beans or cauliflower in place of celery root. This rice pilaf tastes great as a side dish to any of the curries in this book. If you serve just the rice pilaf, arrange bowls of plain yogurt and Indian pickles—mango or lime work best—on the side. You can also serve this dish with chutneys.

Place rice in a medium bowl, wash it well under cold water and drain. Repeat the washing and draining once more. Add the 3¾ cups of water and soak for 20 minutes.

In a medium pot with a lid, combine rice and soaking water, butter and ¾ tsp of the salt on high heat. Once rice starts to boil vigorously, reduce the heat to low, cover and simmer for 12 minutes. Turn off the heat and allow rice to sit, covered, for 8 to 10 minutes. Remove the lid, stir gently and set aside.

Heat oil in a large frying pan on medium-high for 30 seconds. Sprinkle in cumin seeds. Once they start to sizzle, cook for 15 seconds and add onions. Stir well and sauté for 4 to 5 minutes, or until onions are brown on the edges. Add ginger, mushrooms, celery root, the remaining 1 tsp of salt, black pepper and nutmeg and sauté for 4 minutes, or until celery root is cooked yet feels firm, not soft, when you stir it. (Do not overcook celery root, as it will taste like soft turnips.)

Stir the cooked rice and cilantro into the mushroom–celery root mixture.

SERVES 6 AS MAIN DISH
or 8 as a side dish

PREP & COOKING TIME
50 minutes

2 cups white basmati rice

3¾ cups water

1 tsp butter

1¾ tsp salt

⅓ cup cooking oil

1 Tbsp cumin seeds

2 medium onions, finely chopped

1 Tbsp chopped ginger (optional)

1 lb mushrooms, sliced

1½ lbs celery root, peeled and cut in 1-inch dice

½ tsp black pepper

½ tsp nutmeg (optional)

½ cup chopped cilantro

SERVE WITH

Eggplant and Navy Beans in Kalonji and Tamarind Curry

Chicken, Tomato and Green Bean Curry

Oven-baked Chicken and Potatoes in Yogurt and Date Curry

Indian-style Tomato, Onion and Paneer Bruschetta

SERVES 6 TO 8

PREP & COOKING TIME
25 minutes (if you have
already made the paneer)

⅓ cup cooking oil

1 tsp black mustard seeds or
2 tsp cumin seeds (optional)

2 lbs red onions, halved
and then sliced

1 Tbsp chopped garlic
(3 medium cloves)

2 lbs tomatoes
(5 to 6 large), chopped

1 tsp turmeric

2 tsp salt

1 tsp crushed cayenne pepper

½ to ¾ cup chopped cilantro

1 lb paneer (page 52)

1 baguette, sliced in rounds
and toasted (optional)

THIS appetizer is a very simple combination of a tomato-onion-garlic sauté served with paneer (page 52), our homemade cheese. It is our Indian version of Italian bruschetta, and instead of the traditional basil, this recipe calls for cilantro. We also add mustard seeds for colour and a lovely, subtle flavour. You can also use cumin seeds, but since cumin is used in so many other Indian recipes, we recommend the mustard seeds if you have them.

Since juicy, ripe tomatoes are the key to this recipe, make it in the summer or early autumn when these fruits are at their peak. You can use canned whole tomatoes, but the topping will be runnier. Making your own paneer, which takes about an hour and a half from start to finish, takes time but is well worth it. We recommend that you follow the recipe on page 52, but use one gallon of milk and a third of a cup of vinegar since this recipe calls for more paneer. If you're in a hurry, you can buy premade paneer from any Indian grocer.

You can refrigerate any leftover topping, as long as the paneer and tomatoes are separate. Once they are mixed, the paneer loses its texture after four or five hours and becomes almost slimy. The tomatoes will become runnier as well, but the topping should still make for a decent snack the next day.

Heat oil in a frying pan on medium for 1 minute. Add mustard (or cumin) seeds, stir and wait until you hear the first popping sound (or allow cumin seeds to sizzle for 30 seconds). Immediately add onions and sauté for 5 to 8 minutes, or until golden along the edges.

Add garlic and sauté for 1 minute, or until light golden brown. Stir in tomatoes, then add turmeric, salt and cayenne. Stir well and sauté for 4 to 5 minutes, or until tomatoes are warmed through but not mushy and sauce-like. Stir in cilantro.

If you have made your own paneer, chances are that it will be in a round. A pound of paneer will result in fourteen, 2-inch x 2-inch pieces, ¼ to ½ inch high. Not all these pieces will be square, and they don't have to be. Store-bought paneer is easy to cut into squares, but the shape and size of the paneer pieces don't matter as long as you personally like the shape and can serve the pieces easily. Just be sure your paneer is firm. If your paneer is crumbly or soft, or you wish to serve the masala with a baguette, crumble paneer with your hands or chop it into small pieces.

Place a square of paneer on a plate and spoon 1 to 2 Tbsp (or more) of the tomato masala overtop. If paneer pieces are thin enough, layer tomato masala between the pieces, like lasagna. Serve with a knife and fork. To serve with baguette, spread at least 1 Tbsp of tomato masala on each slice of baguette. Place crumbled paneer or small pieces of paneer over the tomato masala. Serve immediately.

SERVE WITH

Any non-paneer dish in this book

Sautéed Spinach and Tomatoes
with Paneer

THIS is our rustic and very quick version of the traditional *saag paneer.* Meeru much prefers this version, as it's not as mellow in terms of spices or as hot in terms of cayenne or jalapeño peppers. It is also much faster to prepare: saag paneer usually takes about two hours to cook.

For this recipe, use as much garlic as you like, but try to follow the measurement for tomatoes, as too many will make the dish too tart. Do make sure the tomatoes are juicy; use diced canned tomatoes if fresh ones are not in season. You can also use fresh or frozen spinach for this dish.

It's better to make the paneer (page 52) beforehand, since it does take time even though it's very easy. If you don't have paneer or don't wish to use it, you can use tofu, tempeh or even chopped potatoes instead. You can also buy ready-made paneer at any Indian grocer.

Serve this spinach as a side dish to any meat or as a second dish to lentils or beans.

Place washed, chopped spinach in a colander and allow any extra water to drain while you cook the masala.

Cut paneer into bite-sized dice and set aside.

Heat oil in a medium pot on medium-high for 45 seconds. Add garlic and sauté for 1 to 2 minutes, or until golden brown. Stir in tomatoes. Add turmeric, salt, cumin, coriander, cloves and cayenne and sauté for 3 to 4 minutes, or until oil glistens on top. Stir in spinach and paneer and mix well. Don't worry if paneer cubes start to crumble. Cover and cook for 2 to 3 minutes, or until spinach has wilted.

SERVES 4 AS A MAIN DISH
or 6 as a side dish

PREP & COOKING TIME
30 minutes (if you have already made the paneer)

1½ lbs fresh spinach (3 bunches) with stems, washed and chopped in ½-inch pieces

10 oz paneer (page 52)

⅓ cup cooking oil

2 Tbsp chopped garlic (6 medium cloves)

1½ cups chopped tomatoes (3 medium)

1 tsp turmeric

1 to 2 tsp salt

1 Tbsp ground cumin

½ Tbsp ground coriander

5 cloves (optional)

1 tsp ground cayenne pepper (optional)

SERVE WITH

Any chickpea or lentil dish in this book

Coconut Curried Chicken

Grilled Beef Tenderloin with Almonds and Garlic (this is a rich combination)

Eggplant and Onions

Sautéed in Cloves and Black Cardamom

SERVES 6

PREP & COOKING TIME
35 minutes

4 black cardamom pods

½ cup cooking oil or ghee

8 cloves

½ tsp asafoetida

1 tsp turmeric

2 lbs eggplant,
cut in ½-inch dice

1½ tsp ground or crushed
cayenne pepper

2 tsp salt

1 medium red onion,
sliced lengthwise

2½ tsp mango powder or
2 tsp tamarind paste (page 42)

½ cup chopped cilantro

THIS dish was inspired by a recent trip to India. While visiting a small town about 110 miles from Jaipur in Rajasthan, Vikram met a young boy on the street. It was late morning, and the boy had heard Vikram asking around for a place to eat *nashta*, a traditional Indian brunch of savoury snacks and chai. With the promise of nashta, the boy led Vikram to his village—a three-mile walk in the heat and dust—and ended up bringing Vikram to his home for lunch.

The boy's mom was happy to include Vikram in the meal, along with her other children, who were seated on the floor by the stove. This was an ages-old, makeshift, one-burner stove fired by dried cow dung and sticks. She made chai, and Vikram enjoyed a simple eggplant dish with chapatti. It wasn't nashta, but it was delicious and it hit the spot.

Eggplant has existed in India even longer than Indians have been using cow dung for fuel. In fact, the first wild eggplant grew in India, and this native Indian eggplant then spread quickly to the rest of Asia. Today, there are many heirloom varieties, and eggplant is one of the most popular staple vegetables throughout the country. Indians love the texture and the many ways it can be prepared: roasted and mashed, grilled, sautéed, and added to a soup-like curry. Eggplant is grown in many sizes, and its colour ranges from white to the dark purple ones we find in Canada and the United States. (As an aside, Thomas Jefferson introduced North Americans to the eggplant.)

Such is India's reverence for its native vegetable that in early 2010, after many protests and a national outcry, the Indian government put a halt to the introduction of a genetically modified, pest-resistant eggplant seed from Monsanto. Although people on both sides of the debate made strong arguments, the main concern for average Indians was that they didn't want any of their eggplant varieties tampered with, fearing that introducing an outside seed manufactured by a large, multinational corporation would mean that India no longer owned its eggplant. Sitting in the boy's hut, Vikram was unaware of any national eggplant controversy, but, coincidentally, he was marvelling at how the eggplant was like a national treasure to all Indians, from those living in huts to those living in mansions.

continued overleaf...

SERVE WITH

Spicy Peas and Mashed
Potato Toasted Sandwiches

Green Cabbage,
Peas and Chicken Curry
on Brown Basmati Rice

Any grilled, seared
or stewed meats

This recipe is Vikram's interpretation of what the young boy's mother made for lunch that day. The dish Vikram ate in Rajasthan was much spicier than this one, and it was cooked in a large *karai*, or heavy Indian wok. If you don't like eggplant, you can use potatoes, fresh pumpkin or any winter squash cut into half-inch dice. We have also made this dish using three chopped mangoes; they will cook in just two minutes, so add them after the onions are mostly cooked. The potatoes, pumpkin and squash will need about the same time as the eggplant. Whichever version you make, serve this dish with a cup of chai and with naan or chapattis.

With a knife, lightly crack the cardamom pods. With your fingers, peel back the shell to release the black seeds and collect them in a small bowl. Discard the shells. With a rolling pin or a mortar and pestle, crush the cardamom seeds (or leave them whole if you don't mind biting into them). Set aside.

Heat oil (or ghee) in a large heavy-bottomed pot or wok on medium-high for 45 seconds. Add cloves and cardamom seeds and sauté for 1 minute. Keeping your head away from the pan, add asafoetida and turmeric, stir, and sauté for 45 seconds. The asafoetida will darken slightly and fall to the bottom of the pan. Immediately stir in eggplant, cayenne and salt and cook, stirring regularly, for 10 minutes. Add onion, stir well and cook for 10 minutes more, or until eggplant has cooked through. Stir in mango powder (or tamarind paste) and cilantro, remove from the heat and serve immediately.

Paneer, Green Beans and Eggplant
in Tamarind Curry

You can play around with this recipe. Make the whole dish as described, or pick and choose your ingredients according to your taste and time. The important flavour components are the onions, tamarind paste, sugar and cumin, and because of the sugar and tamarind, this recipe contains more cumin and mustard seeds than usual. So, you can make this dish without the black mustard seeds; it will still taste good, but it just won't have the same depth of flavour.

Although we've provided recipes for tamarind paste (page 42) and paneer (page 52) in this book, if you are in a hurry, you can buy them at most Indian grocers. Or substitute chopped potatoes for the paneer, but you will have to add them before you would the paneer. Serve this curry as a main dish over rice or with a baguette.

Quickly sift through lentils and discard any stones or dirt. Place lentils in a small frying pan on medium-high heat and stir gently, yet vigorously, with a wooden spoon. (Or hold the frying pan with a cloth and gently toss the lentils over the heat.) As soon as lentils are golden with a few dark edges, 4 to 5 minutes at most, turn off the heat and transfer lentils to a bowl.

Heat oil in the frying pan on medium-high for 30 to 45 seconds and sprinkle in mustard seeds. As soon as they begin to make popping sounds, 1 to 2 minutes, add onions and sauté for 6 to 8 minutes, or until golden brown. Stir in asafoetida and cook for 45 seconds to 1 minute. Reduce the heat to medium and add sugar, cumin, paprika, cayenne, salt and curry leaves. Add tamarind paste, stir well and sauté for 4 to 5 minutes. Stir in lentils and water and bring to a boil. Reduce the heat to medium-low and add eggplant, cover and cook for 8 minutes. Stir in potato (if using instead of paneer), cover and cook for 5 to 10 minutes. Stir in green beans, cover and cook for 5 minutes. Finally, add paneer (if using instead of potato) and continue cooking for 2 minutes so that the paneer is heated through.

SERVES 6

PREP & COOKING TIME
50 minutes (if you have already made or bought the paneer and tamarind paste)

⅓ cup skinless urad lentils (the package will say "washed urad")

½ cup cooking oil

1 Tbsp black mustard seeds

4 cups chopped onions (2 large)

½ tsp asafoetida (optional)

½ cup raw sugar or demerara sugar

3 Tbsp ground cumin

1 tsp paprika

1 Tbsp crushed cayenne pepper

1 Tbsp salt

25 fresh curry leaves

3 Tbsp tamarind paste (page 42)

1½ cups water

1 lb eggplant (1 large), cut in ¾-inch dice

8 to 10 oz paneer (page 52), cut in 1-inch dice, or 13 oz potato (1 large), unpeeled and cut in ¾-inch dice

11 oz green beans, trimmed and cut in 2-inch pieces

SERVE WITH

Quinoa Salad with Lentil Sprouts

Spicy Cauliflower "Steak"

Any lentil curry in this book

Eggplant and Paneer Pâté

ONCE you have made the paneer (page 52) and roasted the eggplant, this dish cooks very quickly. If you're rushed, you can always make these components in advance and refrigerate them, covered, for a day or two. You can also buy paneer from most Indian grocers. And although roasted eggplant tastes great, we've also given the option for making this recipe with unroasted eggplant. (If you roast the eggplant, use only large purple eggplant; if you do not roast the eggplant, any variety is fine.)

Eat this dish with any bread as part of a main meal or even with unflavoured crackers or slices of baguette as a warm hors d'oeuvres.

Roast eggplant, either on your stovetop or in the oven (rub with 1 tsp of the oil), then peel and mash them according to the method on page 50. Alternatively, cut eggplant in 1-inch dice and place them in a colander. Sprinkle eggplant with 1 tsp of the salt and mix thoroughly, then set in the sink to "drain" for 30 minutes. This softens the eggplant (and skin) and shortens the eggplant-cooking time.

Heat the ⅓ cup of oil in a large pot on medium-high for 45 seconds. Add onions and sauté for 4 minutes, or until onions are sweating but not yet browned. Add asafoetida and stir for 45 seconds. Stir in tomatoes, cumin, the ½ Tbsp of salt, turmeric and jalapeño pepper (or cayenne) and sauté for 3 minutes, or until the tomato mixture is sizzling away. Stir in eggplant and paneer and cook for 1 minute if eggplant is roasted and mashed or 6 to 8 minutes if eggplant is diced. (Unless you are watching your salt intake, the salt added to the diced eggplant will not make a noticeable difference in taste.) Mix in cilantro and serve immediately.

SERVES 6

PREP & COOKING TIME
30 minutes + 30 to 45 minutes to roast or drain eggplant (if you have already made the paneer)

2 lbs eggplant

⅓ cup + 1 tsp cooking oil

½ Tbsp + 1 tsp salt

2 cups chopped red onions (1 large)

½ tsp asafoetida (optional)

1 lb tomatoes, chopped (3 large)

1 Tbsp ground cumin

1 tsp turmeric

1 jalapeño pepper, chopped or ½ tsp ground cayenne pepper

8 oz paneer (page 52), cubed or broken into bits

½ cup finely chopped cilantro

SERVE WITH

Any lentil or chickpea dish

Chicken with Crimini Mushrooms and Saffron Curry

Kidney Beans and Rice
(Rajma Chawal)

SERVES 6

PREP & COOKING TIME
30 minutes (if you have
already cooked the rice)

½ cup cooking oil

2 cups chopped onion (1 large)

2 Tbsp finely chopped
garlic (6 medium cloves)

2 Tbsp finely chopped ginger

1½ cups chopped
tomatoes (3 medium)

1½ Tbsp mild
Mexican chili powder

1 tsp turmeric

1 Tbsp ground cumin

1 Tbsp ground coriander

1½ tsp salt

1 tsp black pepper (optional)

1 tsp ground cayenne
pepper (optional)

½ cup plain yogurt,
stirred (optional)

5 to 6 cups water
(6 for a soupier curry)

three 14-oz cans kidney
beans, drained and rinsed

5 to 6 cups cooked white or
brown basmati rice (page 55)

FROM what we've observed, for non-Indian diners kidney beans aren't exactly at the top of the list. In India kidney beans are a staple food item and mightily enjoyed. They're a high source of iron and protein for a vegetarian society. Kidney beans and rice *(rajma chawal)* is as common a combination in India as macaroni and cheese is in North America, and although we speak English at home, we always say "rajma chawal" (pronounced "chavel"), never kidney beans and rice.

When Meeru and Vikram were growing up, rajma chawal was one of our favourite meals, and we introduced it very early into Nanaki and Shanik's diet. It is the one meal that all Indian kids learn how to make when they leave home for good; in fact, as a twenty-year-old student in hotel management in Austria, the one dish that Vikram and his friends could afford to make, and always enjoyed, was rajma chawal. On Sunday afternoons they downed bowls of it along with glasses of cheap whisky.

Meeru's sister, Ritu, didn't put much effort into cooking until her twins got off baby food. At the time the only dish she knew how to make was rajma chawal, so the twins were eating it two to three times a week. Even today all of her recipes are descended from rajma chawal.

When Nanaki was five and Shanik was three, they had some friends over for lunch and wanted to serve rajma chawal. One of the friends saw the kidney beans and said, "Eew, what's that?" Shanik was genuinely bewildered that these kids didn't like this dish. For Nanaki, it was a disappointing moment. It wasn't just that her friends had insulted her favourite food—this meal represented who her family was. For all of Nanaki's pickiness when it comes to Indian food, rajma chawal is still the one she likes most.

continued overleaf...

It may seem silly to write down a rajma chawal recipe for Indians, because most Indians already know how to make it. But this wouldn't be a family cookbook if we didn't include this recipe for those who don't know how to make it and want to come up with their own spice combinations. In our version we add mild Mexican chili powder and less cumin and coriander. In Ritu's version, there are no onions but an abundance of garlic. Ritu and the twins are so hardcore about their rajma that sometimes theirs has only garlic, tomatoes, turmeric, salt and black pepper. If you want to experience the comfort of this dish but really don't like kidney beans, you can also use pinto beans.

To make this recipe quick and easy, we suggest you use canned kidney beans. If you are using soaked dried kidney beans, you will need to boil them on medium heat, covered, for 1 hour. If you are using a pressure cooker to make this dish with dried beans, you will need to cook the beans for 22 to 25 minutes. If you're concerned about having gas at work the next day, there's ginger in the recipe; as long as you chew properly, you'll be fine. For a heartier meal, serve rajma chawal with yogurt or a side salad.

Heat oil in a medium pot on medium-high for 30 seconds. Add onion and sauté for 8 minutes, or until slightly dark brown. Add garlic and sauté for 2 minutes, then stir in ginger and tomatoes. Add chili powder, turmeric, cumin, coriander, salt, black pepper and cayenne and sauté this masala for 5 to 8 minutes, or until oil glistens on top.

Place yogurt in a small bowl. To prevent curdling, spoon about 3 Tbsp of the hot masala into the yogurt. Stir well, then pour yogurt into the pot of masala. Sauté for 2 minutes, or until oil glistens again.

Add water, stir and bring to a boil on high heat. Add kidney beans, stir and bring to a boil again. Reduce the heat to medium and cook for 3 minutes. (If you are using a pressure cooker, you can make the masala in the cooker and then add the dried kidney beans and water.)

Serve the rice and beans buffet-style in separate bowls.

Punjabi Lentil Curry

THE traditional Indian lentils that we use in this recipe are the whole urad lentils, which look like black mung beans. We combine three-quarters urad lentils with one-quarter kidney beans to make this very popular dish. It resembles the *dal mukhani* served in many Indian restaurants. *Mukhani* means buttery, and dal mukhani is usually cooked with whipping cream and butter. We find that urad lentils themselves are quite velvety and buttery and don't need to be hidden behind so much fat, but we add turmeric to our version. Feel free, though, to add a cup of cream at the end of the cooking process. We serve this recipe at both Vij's and Rangoli as our staple side lentil.

If you don't have any urad lentils, you can substitute mung beans in this recipe. You will have a different, non-mukhani flavour, but mung beans still make a hearty dish. If you use mung beans, cook the kidney beans separately or don't use them at all, since they take much longer to cook. Mung beans need no soaking and cook in thirty to forty minutes. (For some reason, we have never made this dish in a pressure cooker, and neither have our mothers.) As well, it only helps to go heavy on the onions and garlic in this dish, since there are few spices.

Serve this lentil curry with a bowl of rice and some yogurt on the side. Or, serve it as a side dish with any meat or vegetable curry.

In a large bowl, combine lentils and kidney beans. Wash and drain them a few times to remove any impurities. Add 6 cups of the water and set aside. Allow lentils and kidney beans to soak for at least 2 hours.

Transfer the lentils, beans and their soaking water to a large pot. Pour in the remaining 7 cups of water, then add asafoetida, salt and turmeric and bring to a boil on high heat. Cover, reduce the heat to low and simmer for 2 hours, stirring occasionally. (These lentils can actually simmer for hours and not lose their taste or texture.)

While the lentils and beans are simmering, in a frying pan, heat butter (or ghee) on medium-low until it melts. Add onion, increase the heat to medium and sauté for 8 to 10 minutes, or until soft and light brown. Add garlic and sauté for 2 minutes. Stir in ginger and jalapeño pepper and sauté for 1 minute. Turn off the heat. Stir the masala into the cooked lentils and beans. Just before serving, stir in cilantro.

SERVES 10

PREP & COOKING TIME
30 minutes + 2 hours to soak the lentils and beans + 2 hours to simmer the lentils and beans

1½ cups whole urad lentils

½ cup dried kidney beans

13 cups water

½ tsp asafoetida

2 tsp salt

1 tsp turmeric (optional)

⅓ to ½ cup butter or ghee

2 cups very finely chopped onion (1 very large)

3 Tbsp chopped garlic (9 medium cloves)

1 Tbsp finely chopped ginger

1 Tbsp finely chopped jalapeño pepper (optional)

¾ cup chopped cilantro

SERVE WITH

Red Bell Pepper, Onion and Sumac Sauté

Sautéed Spinach and Tomatoes with Paneer

Any goat curry (this is a rich combination)

Mung Beans
in Coconut Curry

O̲U̲R daughter Nanaki loves coconut milk and mung beans almost as much as she loves rajma chawal (page 114). Every day for an entire year, she took a thermos of mung beans and brown rice (with nothing but salt and some butter) and ate it for lunch at school. She enjoys anything cooked in coconut milk and especially appreciates it in Indian food since it mellows the spicing. This is a hearty, rich lentil dish that is our family comfort food but not a dinner party dish.

Be careful about the cooking time for the mung beans—they become mushy if they are overcooked, which isn't a taste problem as much as a texture one. In India, whole mung beans are often sprouted and used in salads and aren't eaten as part of a prepared, hot curry. Whole mung beans are very filling, so for *daal* (lentil curry), which is meant to be a lighter dish, split mung beans or split and washed mung beans are cooked instead.

To be honest, we find that non-Indians love this dish more than Indians who are used to eating traditional Indian food. Although we really enjoy this curry, we would never serve it to Vikram or Meeru's parents because they wouldn't like the coconut and lentil combination. Meeru, Nanaki and Shanik eat this curry with brown rice, but for Vikram, a mung bean and brown rice combination is psychologically too healthy sounding to enjoy. He always eats this curry with white basmati rice and some mango pickle or some goat on the side.

Wash and drain mung beans and set aside.

Heat oil in a medium pot on medium-high for 1 minute. Add cumin seeds and allow them to sizzle for 45 seconds, or until they are a darker brown. Add garlic and sauté for 3 to 4 minutes, until brown but not burned. Stir in tomatoes, then add ginger, coriander, turmeric, salt and cayenne. Stir and sauté masala for 5 minutes, or until oil glistens. Add water and mung beans, bring to a boil, then reduce the heat to low, cover and cook for 30 minutes, stirring once or twice. Taste beans to make sure they are cooked.

Stir in coconut milk and increase the heat to medium-high. Bring to a boil and turn off the heat (if you want to thicken your curry some more, you can let it simmer on medium-low heat for 5 to 10 minutes). Stir in cilantro and serve.

SERVES 6 TO 8

PREP & COOKING TIME
1 hour

1 cup mung beans

⅓ cup cooking oil

1 Tbsp cumin seeds

3 Tbsp chopped garlic
(9 medium cloves)

2 cups puréed
tomatoes (4 medium)

2 Tbsp chopped ginger

2 Tbsp ground coriander

1 tsp turmeric

2 tsp salt

½ Tbsp crushed cayenne
pepper (optional)

5 cups water

2 cups coconut milk

½ cup chopped cilantro

SERVE WITH

Spicy Cauliflower "Steak"

Red Bell Pepper and
Shallot Curry

Mango Reduction
Curry with Prawns

Vegetable and Yellow Lentil Curry

SERVES 8

PREP & COOKING TIME
45 minutes

Lentils

1½ cups toor lentils

5 cups water

20 fresh curry leaves

Vegetable curry

¾ oz kokum or ¼ cup
tamarind paste (page 42)

½ cup cooking oil

2 cups chopped onion (1 large)

½ tsp asafoetida

2 Tbsp ground cumin

1 Tbsp salt

1 tsp turmeric

1 tsp ground
cayenne pepper

1½ tsp ground
fenugreek seeds

½ cup chopped
tomato (1 medium)

1 small head of cauliflower,
cut in 1½-inch florets

½ lb green beans, trimmed
and cut in ½-inch pieces

1 cup water

THIS is the closest we've come to making the infamous south Indian staple dish called *sambar*, a slightly tangy (from tamarind and/or kokum) vegetable-lentil curry that is traditionally eaten just about everyday with any meal. Most commonly, it is served with *dosa* (a fermented lentil and rice crêpe) or *idli* (steamed fermented lentil and rice cakes).

When we were travelling through the southern state of Kerala, sambar was served with any lunch or dinner, no matter what we ordered, and at each place the sambar tasted different, so we never got tired of it. Some sambar has fewer lentils and more vegetables, some is very spicy, while other sambar is more tangy. There is no set list of which vegetables to use; basically, it is made from whatever is in season.

In Kerala an Indian vegetable called "drumsticks" is often part of the sambar. Drumsticks look like a thicker version of long green beans, except that their exterior is inedible and you suck and chew the vegetable and spit out the roughage on your plate. This vegetable is absolutely delicious, but initially we found eating it at restaurants very strange. After a few times of sucking and spitting, it was fun and liberating not to worry about being so clean and proper! Drumsticks also add their own flavour to the sambar's stock, so if we ever find a ready supply of them in Vancouver, we'll be tempted to add them to this curry.

In this version we use kokum instead of tamarind for a less tart and more pungent, salty flavour. However, feel free to replace the kokum with tamarind. You can buy these ingredients and the toor lentils at any Indian market. The yellow lentils cook quickly and give the curry a thicker texture than other types of lentils.

You can make this dish ahead of time, but add an additional cup of water to the pot when you reheat it, as the lentils tend to thicken as the curry cools. Serve this particular dish only with white basmati rice, as it doesn't match the flavour of brown rice at all. It also makes a good side dish for any meat or seafood curry.

Lentils Wash and drain the lentils.

Combine lentils, water and curry leaves in a medium pot. Place on high heat and bring to a boil. Reduce the heat to low, cover (leaving a small gap for steam to escape) and cook for 20 minutes. Set aside.

Vegetable curry Spread out the kokum and quickly remove and discard any hard seeds. Chop the skins, pack as many of them as will fit into 1 Tbsp for this recipe and set aside.

Heat oil in a large pot on high for 45 seconds. Add onion and sauté for 8 minutes, or until almost dark brown but not burned. Reduce the heat to medium, add asafoetida and stir well. Add kokum (or tamarind paste), cumin, salt, turmeric, cayenne, fenugreek seeds and tomato, stir well and sauté for 2 minutes. Stir in cauliflower and green beans and sauté for 5 minutes. Pour in water, increase the heat to high and bring to a boil. Reduce the heat to medium, cover and cook for 2 minutes.

Stir in cooked lentils (and their water) and bring to a low boil. Turn off the heat and serve immediately.

SERVE WITH

Roasted Eggplant Raita

Rice Pilaf with Cashews, Cranberries and Saffron

Mango Reduction Curry with Prawns

Dates and Bitter Melon Two Ways

Chickpea and Cucumber Curry

PREP & COOKING TIME
45 minutes (if you use canned
or pre-cooked chickpeas)
+ 30 minutes to cool

Chickpea curry

⅓ to ½ cup cooking oil

12 oz onion (1 large),
halved and sliced

2 Tbsp finely chopped ginger

1 tsp to 1 Tbsp chopped
jalapeño pepper (optional)

1 cup puréed tomatoes
(2 medium)

2 tsp mango powder

1 Tbsp paprika

1 tsp turmeric

1 tsp salt

1 cup water (2 cups if serving
with rice and not as salad)

4 cups cooked chickpeas

1 Tbsp dried green fenugreek
leaves or ½ cup finely
chopped cilantro (optional)

Cucumber

1 lb long English cucumber,
cut in ½-inch dice

¼ tsp black pepper

¼ cup finely chopped
red onion (½ to 1 small)

2 to 3 Tbsp fresh lemon juice

½ to 1 tsp salt

½ cup chopped
cilantro (optional)

SERVE WITH
Serve this dish on its own.

Sometimes in the afternoons, or late at night, we don't want any rice or chapatti. We want Indian food, but we want a light yet filling curry. This chickpea curry is perfect for those occasions. It's actually a warm salad, and once you get the idea, you can add many other ingredients that are in your fridge. In addition to cucumbers, we have used steamed sprouted lentils (which you can buy raw in the produce section and steam at home), diced pears (not the juicy kind) or apples, green bell peppers, carrots, and once, as per Shanik's request, canned corn. You don't need more than a quarter cup per person of additional ingredients.

We serve all the ingredients buffet-style in the middle of the table and allow everyone to make their own salads. There is enough spicing in the chickpeas and cucumber to flavour the other ingredients, but you don't want more than three or four ingredients total; otherwise the spicing becomes bland.

If you want a simple curry with rice, then skip the cucumbers and just make the chickpea curry with an extra cup of water, and serve it piping hot. The amount of jalapeño pepper you use will depend on how spicy yours is. Our measurement is based on a very spicy pepper.

Chickpea curry Heat oil in a medium pot on medium-high for 1 minute. Add onion and sauté for 8 minutes, or until lightly browned. Stir in ginger and jalapeño pepper and sauté for 1 minute. Add tomatoes, mango powder, paprika, turmeric and salt, stir well and cook for 4 to 5 minutes, or until oil glistens on top. Pour in water and chickpeas, stir well and bring to a boil. Reduce the heat to low, cover and simmer for 5 minutes, stirring once or twice. Stir in fenugreek (or cilantro) and allow curry to cool for 30 minutes.

Cucumber In a medium bowl, combine cucumber, black pepper, onion and lemon juice. Mix well and refrigerate, covered, until serving. Add salt and cilantro, toss and serve.

Black Chickpea Pakoras

SERVES 10
(makes 50 to 60 fritters)

PREP & COOKING TIME
2 hours + 6 hours to soak
the chickpeas (or cook dried
chickpeas for 23 to 25 minutes
in a pressure cooker)

1 cup dried black chickpeas

7 cups water

12 oz Russet potato (1 large)

1 cup chickpea flour

1½ cups finely chopped
onion (1 medium-large)

3 Tbsp finely chopped ginger

1 Tbsp salt

1 Tbsp ground cayenne pepper

2 Tbsp ground coriander

2 Tbsp ground cumin

2 cups finely chopped cilantro

1 cup cooking oil for pan-
frying or more for a deep fryer

THIS popular fritter recipe comes from Rangoli and is often featured as one of our vegan dishes but is enjoyed by everyone. We aren't vegans by any means, but we respect that vegans should also enjoy delicious, well-seasoned foods, so most of our vegan dishes rate fairly high on the number of spices and intensity of their flavour.

Ironically, although it's very easy to be a vegan and live off Indian food, vegans in India are almost unheard of. None of us working at Vij's or Rangoli could think of a single Indian-born vegan we know. In fact we wouldn't be surprised to discover that, even with a population of over one billion people, India has fewer vegans than the U.S. or even Canada. The number of vegetarians is a different matter: about half of the Indian population is vegetarian, and this is a sharp decrease from twenty years ago.

Making these pakoras is a labour of love, so cook up a big batch. If you want, you can cut this recipe in half and make 25 to 30 fritters. We serve these fritters three ways: as hors d'oeuvres on their own, with any of the chutneys or even with ketchup; mixed into Yogurt Curry (page 92); or with Coconut Curry for Any Day and Any Dish (page 77). This recipe makes enough pakoras to try them more than one way; however, if you have leftovers, refrigerate them in an airtight container for up to a week or freeze them for up to three weeks. Thaw pakoras and reheat them at 350°F for about fifteen minutes.

Look for black chickpeas and chickpea flour at any Indian grocer. Chickpea flour is also available from many health food stores or gourmet grocers.

Wash and drain chickpeas twice in cold water. Place chickpeas and 3 cups of the water in a medium bowl. Set aside and soak for at least 6 hours or up to 10 hours. (To save time soaking and boiling, you can cook the chickpeas and 6 cups water in a pressure cooker for 23 to 25 minutes.) Place the soaked chickpeas, their water, plus an additional 4 cups of water in a medium pot. Bring to a boil on high heat, reduce heat to medium-low, cover and simmer for 40 to 50 minutes. Carefully taste a chickpea to ensure that it is cooked. Turn off the heat and allow to cool, uncovered, for 30 minutes.

Drain the water from the chickpeas into a clean pot. Reserve this water if you are planning to make the coconut curry or another curry that calls for water; if not, discard it.

Place chickpeas in a blender or food processor and grind to a grainy paste. Add 1 or 2 Tbsp of water if the mixture is too dry and isn't grinding properly. Set aside.

While the chickpeas are boiling, boil the potato as well. Cover potato with water in a medium pot. Place on high heat and bring to a boil. Cover, reduce the heat to medium and boil for 30 to 40 minutes, or until potato is soft when pierced with a knife.

Remove potato from the heat, drain and set it aside to cool. Using a sharp knife or your hands, peel off and discard the skin. Mash the potato, using either your fists or a potato masher. Do not add any water or other liquid when mashing the potato.

continued overleaf...

SERVE WITH

Any of the chutneys
in this book

Coconut Curry for
Any Day and Any Dish

Yam and Tomato Curry

In a large bowl, combine ground chickpeas, mashed potato, chickpea flour, onion, ginger, salt, cayenne, coriander, cumin and cilantro until well mixed.

Scoop 1 Tbsp or more of the chickpea batter into your hands and roll it between your palms to make a thin patty 2½ to 3 inches long, 1½ to 2 inches wide and ½ inch thick. Place it on a large baking sheet. Repeat until you have 50 to 60 fritters.

Line a large baking sheet or a large bowl with paper towels to absorb the oil once the fritters have been fried.

To deep-fry the pakoras, preheat a deep fryer to high. Using a slotted spoon, drop fritters into the deep fryer, making sure to leave room for them to move around. Cook for 1½ minutes, or until crispy on the outside and warmed on the inside. Using the slotted spoon, transfer them to the lined baking sheet (or bowl). Repeat with the remaining fritters.

To pan-fry the pakoras, heat 4 to 6 tsp of oil (1 tsp for each fritter) in a large heavy-bottomed frying pan on high for 1 minute. Add 4 fritters and cook on one side for 2 minutes. Using tongs, carefully turn fritters over and cook for 2 minutes, or until crispy on the outside and warmed on the inside. Using the tongs, transfer them to the lined baking sheet (or bowl). Repeat with the remaining fritters (adding more oil as necessary).

Chickpeas in Star Anise
and Date Masala

THIS is a spicy chickpea dish that we serve as an appetizer at Vij's. The chickpeas are so versatile that we have accompanied them with grilled kale, steamed corn (shaved from the cob) and sautéed cabbage. They taste best with bread and some salted yogurt, even if you serve them with other vegetables or meats. You can also just enjoy them with a bowl of rice.

Drain chickpeas and set aside. With a knife, lightly crack the cardamom pods. With your fingers, peel back the shell to release the black seeds and collect them in a small bowl. Discard the shells. With a rolling pin or a mortar and pestle, crush the cardamom seeds (or leave them whole if you don't mind biting into them). Set aside.

Heat oil in a medium pot on medium-high for 45 seconds. Add onion and sauté for 6 to 7 minutes, or until browned. Stir in garlic and sauté for 1 minute, or until browned. Reduce the heat to medium and stir in tomato paste. Add dates, cumin, salt, cayenne, black pepper, star anise and cardamom seeds and sauté for 2 minutes. Stir in chickpeas and water and heat for 3 to 4 minutes, until masala is well mixed with chickpeas. Turn off the heat and serve immediately.

SERVES 6

PREP & COOKING TIME
30 minutes (if you use canned chickpeas, or once the chickpeas have been soaked overnight and boiled)

three 15-oz cans chickpeas (or 1½ cup raw chickpeas, soaked overnight and boiled)

2 black cardamom pods (optional)

⅓ to ½ cup cooking oil

1½ cups chopped onion (1 medium-large)

2 Tbsp chopped garlic (6 medium cloves)

2½ Tbsp tomato paste

6 fresh or dried dates, pitted and chopped

1 Tbsp + 1 tsp ground cumin

2 tsp salt (or 1 tsp if chickpeas are salted)

1 tsp ground cayenne pepper

1 tsp black pepper (optional)

¼ to ⅓ tsp ground star anise or 2 whole star anise

½ cup water

SERVE WITH

Paneer

Brown Basmati and Portobello Mushroom Pilaf

Eggplant and Navy Beans
in Kalonji and Tamarind Curry

SERVES 4 AS A MAIN DISH
or 6 as a side dish

PREP & COOKING TIME
40 minutes (if you use canned navy beans, or once the beans have been soaked overnight and boiled)

⅓ cup canola oil

1 tsp kalonji seeds

2 cups finely chopped onion (1 large)

1 cup finely chopped tomatoes (2 medium-large)

2 Tbsp ground cumin

2 tsp salt

1 tsp ground cayenne pepper

1 lb eggplant (1 large), cut in ¾-inch pieces

1 cup water

1½ Tbsp tamarind paste (page 42)

one 19-oz can white navy beans, fully drained

SERVE WITH

Brown Basmati Rice

Marinated Duck Breast with Mung Bean and Sesame Seed Rice Pilaf

Fennel and Kalonji-spiced Baby Back Ribs

THIS curry is tangy from the tamarind and a bit toasty from the kalonji seeds. We recommend that you soak and boil raw navy beans to get a better texture (you can also cook the raw navy beans in a pressure cooker for 11 minutes). Canned beans will also work, as long as you rinse and drain them. The risk is that the canned beans can be too mushy. If you like beans, you can add more in the recipe below and decrease the eggplant by a bit—you don't have to be exact, since the spices will work either way.

Meeru likes to mix this dish with plain white basmati rice and turn it into a rice pilaf. You can also serve it as a side dish to any other curry or as a main dish with bread, naan or chapatti on the side.

Heat oil in a large, heavy-bottomed pot on medium-high for about 1 minute. Add kalonji seeds, stir and allow the seeds to sizzle for 20 to 30 seconds. Add onion and sauté for 7 to 8 minutes, or until medium brown. Stir in tomatoes. Stir in cumin, salt and cayenne and sauté for 5 to 8 minutes, or until oil glistens on the masala mixture.

Add eggplant and water and cook on medium heat for 2 to 3 minutes. Stir in tamarind paste, cover and cook for another 10 minutes. Stir in navy beans and remove from the heat.

Celery Root and Bulgur Wheat Koftas
in Tomato and Garam Masala Curry

KOFTAS are fried dumplings traditionally made with grated vegetables, ground meat, paneer and nuts (such as pistachios and cashews) and served in a rich curry. During the period of Mughal rule in India between the sixteenth and nineteenth centuries, meat and paneer koftas with nuts were associated with wealth. Our version has a much healthier vegetarian twist. Celery root and bulgur wheat also give these koftas a lighter flavour and texture. Although koftas use mostly the same ingredients as pakoras, koftas are made with fresh vegetables and ground meats, whereas pakoras are made only with fresh vegetables that are roughly chopped. Koftas can be made with grains such as bulgur and couscous, but pakoras are made with chickpea flour only, which results in lighter, less dense dumplings.

This is a labour-intensive meal that will take about two and a half hours to make. It is well worth the time and effort, however, as it is a very satisfying vegetarian dish that can match any meat curry. We prefer the taste of the curry with whipping cream, but for a vegan recipe, leave out the cream and add more water.

Celery root, which you'll find in the produce section alongside other root vegetables, has a tough and very thick outer skin, so you will need a strong, sharp knife to peel it. Don't worry if you end up with a much smaller and lighter celery root once you have done this. Bulgur wheat is known as *dalia* in Hindi and is available at most Indian grocers, as well as many other grocery stores. Buy either the small or medium grain for this recipe. You can also substitute couscous for the bulgur if you prefer. It is best to deep-fry koftas.

Although we serve the koftas in curry with rice or naan, which is the traditional way, you could also serve them with the curry and some chutneys on the side, as hors d'oeuvres. Freeze any leftover koftas and curry separately in airtight containers for up to a month.

....

Tomato and garam masala curry Heat oil in a medium pot on medium-high for 45 seconds. Add onions and sauté, stirring regularly, for 10 to 15 minutes or until very light brown.

continued overleaf…

continued overleaf…

SERVES 6 TO 8
(makes 36 to 40 koftas)

PREP & COOKING TIME
2 to 3 hours

Tomato and garam masala curry

½ cup cooking oil

2 cups puréed onions
(2 medium)

3 Tbsp finely chopped
garlic (9 medium cloves)

2 cups puréed tomatoes
(4 medium, or canned
is fine in winter)

2 tsp salt

1 tsp turmeric

1 tsp ground cayenne pepper

2 Tbsp garam masala (page 41)

6 cups water (or 7 if you are
not using whipping cream)

1 Tbsp dried green
fenugreek leaves

1½ cups whipping
cream (optional)

Add garlic and sauté, stirring constantly, for 2 to 3 minutes, or until golden brown. Add tomatoes, salt, turmeric, cayenne and garam masala and stir well. Reduce the heat to medium and cook the masala for 8 minutes, or until oil glistens on top.

Add water, stir and bring to a boil. Reduce the heat to medium-low and boil for 15 minutes, or until oil once again glistens on top. Add fenugreek leaves and cream and stir well. Turn off the heat, cover and set aside.

Koftas In a small pan, bring the ¾ cup water and 1 tsp of oil to a boil. Stir in bulgur wheat (if you are using couscous, follow the instructions on the box), turn off the heat, cover and set aside for 10 minutes. Remove the lid and stir. Set aside to cool.

While bulgur wheat (or couscous) is cooling, use a strong, sharp knife to peel the tough, thick skin off celery root. Wash celery root under cold running water and pat it dry with a paper towel. Use a box grater to grate celery root into a large bowl. Stir in bulgur wheat (or couscous), onion, ginger, cilantro, cayenne, salt, turmeric and chickpea flour. Using your hands, mix thoroughly until well combined. The moisture in the celery root will make the mixture sticky enough to hold together.

Scoop 1½ to 2 Tbsp of the kofta batter into your hands and roll it between your palms to make a ball about 1½ inches in diameter. (You may need to rub some oil on your hands.) Place it on a large baking sheet. Repeat until you have 36 to 40 balls.

Line a baking sheet with a double layer of paper towels.

Preheat a deep fryer to high. Using a slotted spoon, drop kofta balls into the deep fryer. (Cook the koftas in several batches so that you don't overcrowd them.) Fry for 3 to 4 minutes, or until golden brown on the outside, with specks of dark brown. Transfer cooked koftas to the lined baking sheet. Repeat with the remaining koftas. Once all koftas are cooked, gently pat tops of koftas with paper towels to soak up any additional oil.

Just before serving, reheat curry on medium until it starts to boil gently. Place koftas in the curry and serve.

Koftas

¾ cup water

1 tsp cooking oil

½ cup small- or medium-grain bulgur wheat or couscous

3 lbs celery root

½ cup finely chopped onion (1 small)

3 Tbsp finely chopped ginger

½ cup chopped cilantro

1 Tbsp + 1 tsp crushed cayenne pepper

1½ tsp salt

1 tsp turmeric

1 cup chickpea flour

cooking oil for deep-frying

SERVE WITH

Roasted Eggplant Raita (on the side)

Red Bell Pepper, Onion and Sumac Sauté (on the side)

Any of the rice pilafs in this book

SEAFOOD

GIVEN THE DISMAL situation of the world's fisheries and oceans from overfishing and overconsumption of seafood, we strongly request that you refer to the various sustainable seafood websites before purchasing fish and shellfish. Before we use any seafood, we ask where it came from, how it was caught and whether it is in abundant supply and not threatened. It's very simple to know which seafood is okay to eat and which is not: just type "sustainable seafood guide" or "sustainable seafood choices" in your Internet search engine, and you will get various reputable websites from Blue Ocean Institute, Environmental Defense Fund, Monterey Bay Aquarium, Marine Stewardship Council, SeaChoice, Ocean Wise, and so on.

Since we're based in Vancouver, British Columbia, we cook a lot with B.C. sablefish and spot prawns and have included some recipes in this book because we know they're responsibly managed, sustainable seafood. If you don't have access to trap-caught spot prawns or California-farmed prawns, don't buy imported farmed or wild prawns, as they come from countries with very few environmental regulations. Warm-water shrimp farms are very crowded, depend on antibiotics and other chemicals to maintain "disease-free" populations or frequently have high levels of fecal content in their water. The farms often release these chemicals and waste products into already sensitive coastal environments.

Wild-caught imported prawns are fished by bottom trawling, which involves dragging a large weighted net behind a boat to catch the shrimp that are churned up from the ocean bottom. Unfortunately, lots of other fish and shellfish, along with already endangered sea turtles, are unnecessarily caught and killed when they get swept up in the nets.

Not only is eating the wrong seafood harmful to our environment, but increasingly it's harmful to our personal health, too—we hear warnings of mercury levels in the news more often now. Most sustainable seafood guides point out these health factors as well. In the end it really isn't that difficult to identify which seafood is good to eat—from both environmental and personal health perspectives. The organizations mentioned above list and continually update information on their websites about which seafood is fine for consumption, and you can even download these lists on wallet-size cards to take shopping with you. Many restaurants, grocery stores and seafood vendors are also becoming aware of these issues. Armed with good sources of information and conscientious sellers, most likely you'll find the right seafood choice and help spread the word about sustainable seafood.

Spicy Roasted Crickets

SERVES 4 TO 6

PREP & COOKING TIME
20 minutes +
20 minutes to cool

100 four-week-old
frozen crickets

1 tsp cooking oil

½ tsp salt

1 tsp ground cumin or
garam masala (page 41)

½ tsp ground cayenne pepper

CRICKETS are members of the same family as prawns. We don't expect that many people will actually source crickets and make this dish, but putting crickets on our menu at Vij's led to one of the most interesting years of our professional lives. For one year, we offered a *parantha* (flatbread) made from spiced, roasted and ground crickets. The flatbread recipe is complicated and very time consuming, but this recipe is much easier. It's as simple as roasting almonds or cashews, and you can eat these spiced, roasted crickets just as you would eat spiced nuts.

Before we got started, and to learn more about eating bugs, we invited David George Gordon, a bug cookbook author, biologist and entomophagist (someone who studies the value of eating insects) to meet us for dinner in Vancouver. He drove up from Seattle with a mind full of facts and a cooler full of bugs, and his enthusiasm for promoting insects as food was intimidating, intoxicating and rational. He also confirmed that, until specialty food stores sell edible insects along with other gourmet products, the best place to buy a small quantity of them is the pet store. (David buys all of his insects from Fluker Farms in Louisiana—they provide shipping.) Look for four-week-old crickets, as the six-week-old ones are quite large.

We needed quite a lot of crickets to make our paranthas, so we located Reeves Cricket Ranch in Everson, Washington. We discovered that the crickets were raised on an apple feed (if you're concerned, many pet stores write down what the bugs are fed), and we had our crickets tested by the Vancouver health department to be sure they were absolutely fine for human consumption.

When Meeru first made this cricket recipe, Vikram's sister and her two young sons were visiting from Singapore. The boys embraced the idea of eating bugs but were surprised that they tasted good. At first Nanaki and Shanik refused to try them. Shanik was in the third grade at the time, and a boy in her class was teasing and chasing her. When she realized that she could impress this boy (and scare him as well) by eating crickets, she gave them a try and took some to school. Many of our customers were both shocked and curious about our decision to put crickets on the menu, and Vikram thoroughly enjoyed the look on their faces—before ordering the crickets and after having eaten them. The insect paranthas were very popular.

If you decide to make this dish, you can buy the live crickets from your local pet store and put them in your freezer. Apparently, this is the most painless way for the insects to die. (It's much easier and cleaner even than trimming fat off of beef, lamb, chicken.) For an extra protein and iron boost, roast the crickets without the salt or spices, grind them in a spice (or coffee) grinder and add them to bread, cookie and muffin recipes.

Be sure to use only fresh crickets and store them carefully. Do not eat raw crickets (just as you would never eat uncooked poultry), and try to consume roasted ones within the day. If you do have some roasted crickets or roasted and ground crickets left over, they will keep refrigerated in an airtight container for a day or two.

SERVE WITH

Serve this dish on its own (as an hors d'oeuvre).

Preheat the oven to 350°F.

Spread crickets on a baking sheet, sprinkle with oil, salt, cumin (or garam masala) and cayenne, and toss until thoroughly mixed. Bake for 15 minutes, stirring once halfway through, or until darker, crunchy and dry but not black and burned. Roast them for another 5 minutes, if necessary. Allow to cool for 20 minutes, then serve within a few hours.

Steamed Sablefish

I N this recipe, you can use as many or as few spices as you choose, but be sure to use the oil and salt. Sablefish has a strong flavour, so it can easily stand on its own. We prefer to eat sablefish with the skin on.

....

In a large bowl, combine oil with fennel seeds, cumin, salt and cayenne. Add sablefish and mix gently. (You don't need to marinate this fish because it's such a buttery, strong-flavoured fish that too much marinating actually takes away from its flavour.)

Bring water to a boil in a large double boiler with a steamer insert on high heat. (If you don't have a double boiler, try setting a metal colander inside a large pot with a lid. Fill the pot with about 1 inch of water; the water should not touch the fish.) Place sablefish in the top part of the double boiler, ensuring that the fish pieces do not overlap. (Steam sablefish in two or three batches, if necessary, to prevent overcrowding). Cover and steam sablefish for 5 minutes, or until fish flakes easily when gently poked with a knife. Remove from the heat.

SERVES 6

PREP & COOKING TIME
15 minutes

¼ cup cooking oil

1 Tbsp + 1 tsp ground fennel seeds (page 78, optional)

1 Tbsp + 1 tsp ground cumin (optional)

1 tsp salt

1 tsp ground cayenne pepper

1½ lbs boneless sablefish, skin on, cut in 2½-inch dice

SERVE WITH

Green Beans, Potatoes and Spinach in Coconut Curry

Coconut Vegetable Curry

Mango Reduction Curry with Prawns (with or without the prawns) and Celery and Navy Bean Salad (as a full meal)

Mango Reduction Curry
with Prawns

SERVES 6

PREP & COOKING TIME
1 hour

Mango reduction

⅓ cup cooking oil

2 cups finely chopped onion (1 large)

¼ cup ghee or cooking oil

2 Tbsp + 1 tsp yellow mustard seeds

2 Tbsp + 1 tsp cumin seeds

1 tsp kalonji seeds

1 cup finely chopped tomatoes (2 medium-large)

1½ tsp salt

2 Tbsp ground coriander

1 Tbsp crushed cayenne pepper

5 cups pure mango juice

Prawns

1 tsp salt (optional)

1½ lbs medium to large prawns (about 36), peeled

6 Tbsp cooking oil (optional)

SOMETIMES, finding a new recipe to replace an already popular and delicious one on the menu can be very frustrating. If the new recipe isn't as good or better than the old one, then our regular customers let us know. Sital, Amarjeet and Meeru had spent many unsuccessful afternoons trying to come up with a new seafood recipe. After using every spice they could think of, Meeru joked out of frustration, "Just toss some fish in a bowl of mango juice, since that's the only thing left." Sure enough, we threw in some prawns and this recipe was born. At Vij's, we have served this mango reduction with B.C. halibut, B.C. sablefish and California-farmed prawns or local B.C. spot prawns, so choose whichever seafood you prefer.

Although it has a fresh and crisp flavour, this curry is nevertheless quite rich. In this recipe, be sure to use yellow mustard seeds and not the black ones. The flavour of almost-burned sautéed onions is also important. Because mango juice is sweet, we have used more cayenne than usual; however, if you wish you can cut this amount in half. Finally, we use a thick mango juice rather than a watery kind—usually the Indian or South African brands of mango juices work best.

Mango reduction Heat oil in a large, heavy-bottomed pan on high for 1 minute. Add onions and sauté, stirring regularly, for 5 to 8 minutes, or until dark brown. Remove from the heat and set aside.

Heat the ¼ cup ghee (or oil) in a medium pot on medium-high for 45 seconds. Add mustard, cumin and kalonji seeds all at once and heat them, stirring constantly, for 1 to 2 minutes, or until you hear the first few popping sounds. (The stirring will make a squeaky noise.) Add tomatoes and stir to combine. Add salt, coriander and cayenne and cook, continuing to stir well, for another 4 to 5 minutes, or until ghee (or oil) is glistening. Add mango juice and bring the mixture to a boil. Reduce the heat to medium and allow it to boil gently, uncovered, for 5 minutes until the ghee (or oil) once again glistens on top.

Balance a fine-mesh sieve or a strainer with handles over the pan of sautéed onions. Be sure that it's well balanced and sturdy. Carefully pour mango reduction curry into the sieve (or strainer) and allow it to drain into the onions. Using a large ladle or a cooking spoon, press tomatoes and spices to extract as much liquid and flavour as possible, then discard the solids.

Prawns To make crispy prawns, rub salt gently all over prawns. In a large frying pan or wok, heat oil on medium-high for 45 seconds. Add prawns, stirring and sautéing for about 4 minutes, or until they are just pinkish-orange all over. Be sure not to overcook the prawns. You can either put cooked prawns in the curry or place the prawns in a dish and pour hot curry overtop to serve.

Alternatively, if you prefer not to use any oil, simply add prawns (with or without the salt) to the simmering mango reduction and cook for about 4 minutes, or until they are pink. Again, be sure not to overcook the prawns.

SERVE WITH

Brown Basmati Rice OR Spinach and Split Pea Mash

Celery and Navy Bean Salad

Eggplant and Onions Sautéed in Cloves and Black Cardamom

Dates and Bitter Melon Two Ways (vegetarian version)

Prawns in Pomegranate Curry

SERVES 6

PREP & COOKING TIME
20 minutes (or longer if
you need to devein the prawns)

36 to 42 prawns
(6 or 7 prawns per person)

1½ tsp salt

½ cup ghee or cooking oil

1 Tbsp cumin seeds

3 cups finely chopped red
onions (3 medium)

1 tsp turmeric

1 tsp ground cayenne
pepper or black pepper

1 tsp chopped jalapeño pepper

1 Tbsp finely chopped ginger

½ cup pomegranate
or mango juice

½ cup chopped cilantro

SERVE WITH

Celery, Tomato and
Green Onion Sauté

Turnips and Tomatoes
in Kalonji Masala

Any of the rice pilafs
in this book

Our brother-in-law, Gregg, made this recipe on his mini-stove in New York City. He banished us all from the kitchen, then emerged twenty-five minutes later with the finished dish. When we sat down to taste his curry, we all agreed that it wasn't very good at all, and all eyes were on Meeru's faulty recipe. But the recipe was fine.

Most of the recipes in this book are very forgiving, but this one has very few ingredients, so each one counts. Following Meeru's cardinal rule that nothing (for the most part) in Indian cooking is carved in stone, Gregg had chopped three onions into large pieces and cooked them according to this recipe. The result was a weak, sweet masala. To obtain the desired robust, browned onion flavour and thick-textured masala, it's crucial that you finely chop the onions in this recipe. If you insist on chopping the onions in large pieces, then you will have to double or triple your sautéing time.

You *can* vary the juice in this recipe, if you like. The pomegranate juice will have more of a zing (which we prefer), and mango juice will make the dish slightly sweeter. If you have any leftover juice, add shots of vodka and ice to it and drink as an aperitif to set a festive mood for dinner. Serve with slices of baguette or bowls of rice.

Peel prawns and devein them, if required. Gently rub prawns with ½ tsp of the salt, place them in a bowl and refrigerate them if you're not going to cook them right away.

In a large frying pan, heat ghee (or oil) on medium-high for 1 minute. Sprinkle in cumin seeds and allow them to sizzle for 45 seconds. Add onions and sauté for 8 minutes, or until golden brown with darker edges. Reduce the heat to medium and add turmeric, the remaining 1 tsp of salt and cayenne (or black pepper). Stir, sauté for 1 minute, then add jalapeño pepper and ginger and sauté for 1 minute more.

Add pomegranate (or mango) juice and bring it to a boil, which will take less than 30 seconds. Add prawns and stir gently. Sauté prawns—still stirring gently—for about 4 minutes, or until orange-pink and firm when poked with a spoon. Remove from the heat and stir in cilantro.

Tilapia
in Yogurt and Ginger Curry

YOGURT can be a good alternative to onions and garlic. We don't mean that they are similar in flavour, but yogurt is bold enough to carry a curry without the aid of onions and garlic. So, make this dish if you don't like onions or garlic or if you want a change from regular onion-based curries. You can just as easily add sautéed onions or garlic to this dish if you like, or not use ginger at all. This curry is a lighter version of Yogurt Curry (page 92).

At Rangoli, we serve variations of this curry with spiced, breaded and seared tilapia. You could use any white fish, but please make sure that the fish comes from a sustainable farm and that, if it's wild, it isn't an endangered or threatened fish. Buy the fillets boned, trimmed and scaled, or, if you prefer, buy the entire fish and prepare it yourself at home. If you're a vegetarian, you can serve just the curry as a soup with rice on the side. You can also sauté your favourite vegetables in some oil with salt and mix them with the rice and curry.

We always serve this dish with white basmati rice in a large bowl.

Yogurt and ginger curry Place yogurt in a large bowl and set aside.

In a medium pot, heat oil on medium for 1 minute. Add cumin seeds and allow them to sizzle for 30 to 45 seconds, or until darker brown. Stir in asafoetida. It will sizzle within 30 to 45 seconds and darken, which means it is cooked. Add ginger, stir and sauté for 1 minute. Add salt, turmeric, coriander, paprika and cayenne and stir for 2 to 3 minutes. The spices will become slightly pasty. Turn off the heat and stir in water.

To prevent the yogurt from curdling, whisk 1 cup of the masala-water mixture into the yogurt. Pour the yogurt into the pot of masala-water and stir well with a whisk. Turn the heat to high and bring curry to a boil, whisking constantly, then reduce the heat to medium-low and simmer for 5 minutes, stirring once or twice. Set aside while you prepare the fish.

continued overleaf…

continued overleaf…

SERVES 6

PREP & COOKING TIME
30 minutes

Yogurt and ginger curry

2 ½ cups plain yogurt (minimum 2% milk fat), stirred

⅓ cup cooking oil

1 ½ tsp cumin seeds

¼ tsp asafoetida (optional)

3 Tbsp finely chopped ginger

1 ½ tsp salt

1 tsp turmeric

2 Tbsp ground coriander

1 Tbsp paprika

1 tsp ground cayenne pepper (optional)

3 cups water

½ cup chopped cilantro

< *shown here with Beet Greens Sautéed in Ginger, Lemon and Cumin, page 63*

145

Pan-seared breaded tilapia

6 whole fillets or 12 boned
and trimmed fillets tilapia
(1½ to 2 lbs total), skin on

½ cup bread crumbs

1 tsp ground cayenne pepper

1 tsp salt

2 Tbsp ground coriander

½ tsp turmeric

½ tsp black pepper (optional)

1 tsp paprika (optional)

½ tsp asafoetida (optional)

6 to 8 tsp cooking oil

SERVE WITH

Spinach and Split Pea Mash

Spicy Cauliflower "Steak"

Red Bell Pepper
and Shallot Curry

Pan-seared breaded tilapia If necessary, trim whole fillets by placing them on a cutting board and, using a large knife, cutting off and discarding the skimpy, whitish edges that are mostly skin (about ¼ inch each side). Scrape any fish scales off the skin and discard them (there shouldn't be too many on tilapia). And, if necessary, cut each fillet lengthwise down the middle and check for bones. You can usually cut them out quite easily by slicing a lengthwise V into the bones and pulling them out. You can also feel with your hands to see if there are any bones or scales still on the fish and pull out with your hands any that are left over. Wash the fillets and set them aside in a colander to dry for a few minutes. You should have a total of 12 small fillets.

In a large bowl, combine bread crumbs, cayenne, salt, coriander, turmeric, black pepper, paprika and asafoetida. Add tilapia fillets and mix carefully until fish is coated with the spiced bread crumbs.

Heat 1 tsp oil in a heavy-bottomed frying pan on medium for 1 minute. Place 2 fillets, skin side down, in the frying pan and cook for about 2 minutes. (If the fillets begin to burn or stick to the pan, add a bit more oil.) Gently turn the fish over and cook the second side for 2 minutes, or until flesh flakes when gently poked with a knife. Transfer the cooked fillets to a baking sheet. Add 1 tsp oil to the frying pan, heat for 1 minute, then cook 2 more fillets. Repeat with the remaining fillets.

Finish curry Heat curry on high and bring to a boil, stirring 2 to 3 times. Stir in cilantro and serve piping hot over tilapia fillets.

Steamed Marinated Halibut

OFTEN we visit our friends Victoria and Oleg's home for Ukrainian dinner, and Victoria serves us steamed crab and other fish with various dressings made from mayonnaise, horseradish and garlic. Luckily, we really enjoy Victoria and Oleg's company, so we don't have to pretend to be their friends just to eat their delicious Ukrainian food.

This is our Indian version of Victoria's steamed fish, using local halibut with our sour cream Indian dressing (page 43). We recommend that you serve this dish with the sour cream dressing or even just mayonnaise, but if you choose not to, we suggest a squeeze of lemon on the steamed halibut.

Combine halibut, oil, salt, cayenne and garam masala (or cumin) in a large bowl. Toss lightly to coat the fish, then cover and refrigerate for 1 to 3 hours to allow halibut to marinate.

Bring water to a boil in a large double boiler with a steamer insert on high heat. (If you don't have a double boiler, try setting a metal colander inside a large pot with a lid. Fill the pot with about 1 inch of water; the water should not touch the fish.) Place halibut in the top part of the double boiler, ensuring that the fish pieces do not overlap. (Steam halibut in two or three batches, if necessary, to prevent overcrowding). Cover, reduce the heat to medium-high and steam halibut for 4 minutes, or until fish flakes easily when gently poked with a knife. Remove from the heat.

SERVES 8

PREP & COOKING TIME
15 minutes + 1 to 3 hours to marinate the fish (if you have already made the dressing)

2 lbs skinless and boneless halibut, cut in 2-inch dice

⅓ cup cooking oil

1 tsp salt

1 tsp ground cayenne pepper

1 to 2 tsp garam masala (page 41) or ground cumin

SERVE WITH

Coconut Curry for Any Day and Any Dish

Ground Fennel Seed Curry

Yam and Tomato Curry

Steamed Marinated Halibut

in Black Chickpea, Potato and Coconut Curry

SERVES 6

PREP & COOKING TIME
2 hours + 6 hours to
soak the chickpeas

Black chickpeas

1 cup dried black
chickpeas

9 cups water

½ tsp salt

WE love the combination of halibut and black chickpeas and will most likely keep coming up with different recipes based on these two ingredients. In this recipe we combine a steamed halibut with a rich curry. To bring out the flavours of garlic and ginger, we chop the onion as finely as the garlic so that it's less dominant. We also use the usual curry spices in this dish, but with one rare omission—turmeric. This combination of ingredients just doesn't need it. Finally, we marinate the halibut in any oil but olive, as olive oil has a stronger flavour than many other oils. This is a full-on recipe that will take you time to prepare, so try not to skip out on any of the ingredients, except for adjusting the salt and cayenne to your taste.

Punjabi food folklore has it that the water from soaking black chickpeas is full of health benefits and should always be used for cooking. Our moms still do this, as their moms and many generations of moms did before them. We follow this tradition, even at our restaurants, by using this reserved soaking water in our curries. Having said that, it is not essential that you follow this tradition.

We prefer to steam the halibut in this dish in a double boiler for a few minutes rather than searing it, as the extra oil needed for searing adds weight to this dish, and the potato-coconut curry is already quite rich. If you don't have a double boiler, try setting a metal colander inside a large pot with a lid. Be sure not to add too much water to the pot; you want to steam the fish, not boil it.

Even though this is a complicated recipe, serve it simply with rice, a green salad, or carrot sticks and cucumber rounds on the side.

Black chickpeas Wash and drain the chickpeas twice in cold water. Place chickpeas and 3 cups of the water in a medium bowl. Set aside and allow to soak for at least 6 hours or up to 10 hours. (To save time soaking and boiling, you can cook the chickpeas and 6 cups water in a pressure cooker for 23 to 25 minutes.)

Drain the soaking water into a clean pot. Reserve this water for the curry.

Combine chickpeas and the remaining 6 cups of water in a medium pot on high heat. Add salt and bring to a boil, then reduce the heat to low, cover and simmer for 40 to 50 minutes. (Taste a chickpea to see if it is cooked.)

Turn off the heat. You should have approximately 4 cups of water left in the pot of chickpeas. If you don't have enough, add some of the reserved chickpea soaking water to make 4 cups.

Halibut While the chickpeas are cooking, gently combine halibut, oil, salt and cayenne in a medium bowl. Cover and refrigerate while you make the curry. (You can also marinate the halibut up to 24 hours in advance and keep it, covered, in the refrigerator.)

Coconut curry Heat oil in a medium-large pot on medium-high for 1 minute. Add onion and sauté for 4 minutes, then add garlic and sauté for 1 minute. Stir in ginger, tomato, salt, paprika, cayenne, cumin and coriander and sauté for 4 to 5 minutes, or until spices become a bit pasty and stick slightly to the bottom of the pot. Stir in potato, coconut milk and cooked chickpeas and their water. Reduce the heat to medium-low, cover and cook while you steam the halibut. In the final few minutes, stir in mint (or fenugreek).

Finish halibut Bring water to a boil in the bottom of a double boiler. Loosely arrange halibut in a single layer in the top of the double boiler (you may need to steam the fish in two or three batches). Set the top of the double boiler over the boiling water, cover and steam for 4 minutes. Remove the cover and gently poke one piece of fish gently with a knife to see if it flakes easily. The fish should be white but not hard to the touch. Steam halibut another minute or two, if necessary. Transfer cooked fillets to a plate. Repeat with the remaining halibut.

Place the halibut in a bowl and top it with piping hot curry.

Halibut

2 lbs skinless and boneless halibut, cut in 2-inch dice (about 24 pieces)

⅓ cup cooking oil

1 tsp salt

1 tsp ground cayenne pepper

Coconut curry

⅓ cup cooking oil

2 cups finely chopped onion (1 large)

2 Tbsp chopped garlic (6 medium cloves)

2 Tbsp finely chopped ginger

½ cup chopped tomato (1 medium)

2 tsp salt

2 tsp paprika

2 tsp ground cayenne pepper

1 Tbsp ground cumin

1 Tbsp ground coriander

1 large potato, boiled and roughly mashed

2 cups coconut milk

1 Tbsp dried mint or dried green fenugreek leaves (optional)

SERVE WITH

Serve this dish on its own.

Grilled Marinated Wild Salmon
in Green Onion, Coconut and Ginger Broth

SERVES 6 TO 8

PREP & COOKING TIME
1 hour to make the broth
only; 1½ hours to make
salmon in broth + 3 hours
to marinate salmon

Marinated salmon

⅓ cup cooking oil

⅓ cup fresh lemon juice

1 tsp salt

½ tsp ground cayenne pepper

1 Tbsp paprika

1 Tbsp garam masala
(page 41) or ground cumin

2½ lbs boneless salmon, skin
on, cut in 16 to 18 equal pieces

**Green onion, coconut
and ginger broth**

6 cups water (or 7 cups if
you prefer a soupier broth)

10 oz potatoes (3 small),
peeled and halved

4 Tbsp finely chopped ginger

½ cup ghee or butter

1 Tbsp + 1 tsp cumin seeds

½ tsp asafoetida

2 bunches green onions
(about 14 stalks), white and
green parts, finely chopped

½ cup finely chopped
tomato (1 medium-large)

2 Tbsp finely chopped
jalapeño pepper

1 Tbsp salt

3 cups coconut milk

WE recommend you use wild salmon to make this recipe because, unlike the enclosed farms used to raise other fish, salmon farms are coastal, and many marine environmental groups and scientists have questioned the farming practices as well as the impact salmon farms have on the oceans. Given the shape of the fish, it may be difficult to cut equal-sized pieces of salmon, but try to keep them similar enough that they cook in the same amount of time.

The broth in this recipe is lighter and more mildly spiced than most curries—in fact the flavour of the ghee stands out, since we don't use many other spices. We based the measurement for the jalapeño pepper on a medium-spicy pepper, but adjust the amount based on your preference and the strength of your pepper. To test its heat, cut open the pepper, tap it with your finger and then lick your finger. If it is a very spicy pepper, you will taste it right away and you can reduce the amount to one tablespoon.

In addition to serving this broth with the salmon, you can also serve it like a soup on its own (with just a piece of baguette).

Marinated salmon In a large bowl, combine oil, lemon juice, salt, cayenne, paprika and garam masala (or cumin) until well mixed. Add salmon and stir gently until fish is well coated with the spice mixture. Cover with plastic wrap and refrigerate for 3 hours.

Green onion, coconut and ginger broth In a large pot, combine water, potatoes and ginger and bring to a boil on high heat. Reduce the heat to low, cover and boil for 30 to 45 minutes, or until potatoes are cooked. Turn off the heat and set aside (do not drain potatoes).

In a heavy-bottomed pan, heat ghee (or butter) on medium-high for 1 minute. Sprinkle in cumin seeds and allow to sizzle for about 15 seconds. Sprinkle in asafoetida and cook for 15 seconds more. Add green onions and sauté for 5 to 6 minutes, or until dark brown but not burned. Stir in tomato, jalapeño pepper and salt and cook for 4 to 5 minutes, or until ghee starts to glisten. Turn off the heat and set aside.

Transfer potatoes from the pot to a large bowl, reserving the ginger broth, and mash until smooth (you can add a bit of ginger broth, but do not add any milk). Stir mashed potatoes into the green onion and tomato masala. Using a large ladle, spoon ginger broth into the masala, stir well,

then add coconut milk. Stir again and turn heat to medium-high and bring to a boil. Reduce the heat to low and boil gently, stirring regularly, for 10 minutes, or until ghee glistens on top.

Finish salmon Heat a barbecue or stovetop grill to high. Place 3 pieces of salmon on the grill. Using tongs, turn salmon each minute for a total of 5 to 6 minutes, or until fish flakes easily when gently poked with a knife. Transfer cooked salmon pieces to a clean plate. Repeat with the remaining salmon, until all pieces are cooked. Serve salmon in bowls with 1 to 1½ cups of broth per person.

SERVE WITH

Rice Pilaf with Cashews, Cranberries and Saffron

Baked Jackfruit in Garlic Marinade (this is a rich combination; as a side for a dinner party)

Eggplant and Paneer Pâté (this is a rich combination; as a side for a dinner party)

Dungeness Crab Spoons
with Coconut, Cilantro and Jalapeño Peppers

THIS dish is one of Vikram's most elegant recipes. It combines a myriad of spices that offer a gentle yet exotic hint of flavour. You don't have to use all of them, but to make the most of the Dungeness crab, do try to use whichever ones you can. You will need a two-foot square of cheesecloth or another similar type of muslin cloth to infuse the crab. Keep a little extra jalapeño pepper, lemon and cilantro on hand, in case you want to add a bit more after you've mixed all the ingredients together.

At Vij's we serve this crab mixture on various large soup spoons, using one tablespoon per serving. You don't have to be exact in your measurements, though, since it's easy to eat more than one spoon per person. Soup spoons that can sit on their own are perfect for this recipe.

In a medium pot, combine water, turmeric, ½ tsp of the salt, fennel seeds, cardamom, cloves, peppercorns, kalonji, ginger, mace and cayenne. Bring to a boil on high heat and then reduce to medium. Cover and boil for at least 20 minutes or up to ½ hour for a stronger flavour. Turn off the heat and allow the stock to cool until it is just warm to the touch.

While the stock is cooling, arrange the cheesecloth (or muslin) on a clean work surface. Grasp the left-hand edge of the cheesecloth and fold it one-third of the way over the rest of the cheesecloth. Repeat with the right-hand edge of the cheesecloth to create a piece of cheesecloth that is three layers thick. Place crabmeat in the cheesecloth, gather the four corners and tie them together with a piece of kitchen string so that no crabmeat can escape.

Set a large sieve over a medium bowl or a clean pot. Gently strain the stock through the sieve and discard the solids. Place the crabmeat sachet into the stock and allow it to infuse for 1 hour.

Remove the sachet from the stock and squeeze it gently to remove any excess water. Carefully untie the sachet. In a medium bowl, combine crabmeat, jalapeño pepper, the remaining ¼ tsp of salt, cilantro, lemon juice and coconut cream (or coconut milk). Taste the mixture and adjust the seasoning until you have mild flavours of coconut, cilantro, lemon and peppers. Cover and refrigerate the crab mixture until just before serving. Will keep refrigerated for up to 3 days.

To serve, arrange twelve to fourteen soup spoons on a serving platter. Drop one tablespoonful of the crab mixture into each soup spoon.

SERVES 6 TO 8

PREP & COOKING TIME
1 hour + 1 hour to infuse crab

6 cups water

¼ tsp turmeric

¾ tsp salt

1 Tbsp fennel seeds

5 green cardamom pods, lightly pounded

8 cloves

½ tsp black peppercorns

½ tsp kalonji seeds

1 tsp chopped ginger

¼ tsp whole, pounded mace (optional)

4 whole dried cayenne peppers (optional)

9 ½ oz Dungeness crabmeat, picked for bits of shell and cartilage

1 to 2 tsp finely chopped jalapeño pepper

¼ cup finely chopped cilantro

1 Tbsp fresh lemon juice

2 Tbsp coconut cream or very thick coconut milk

SERVE WITH

Celery and Navy Bean Salad and Baked Jackfruit in Garlic Marinade (as part of an appetizer platter)

Turnips and Tomatoes in Kalonji Masala

POULTRY

SEVERAL YEARS AGO we realized the conventional chicken we were buying was worthless in terms of nutrients and flavour and most likely unhealthy. The main reason conventional chicken is so inexpensive is that the birds are raised in factory farms that keep them in horrid, extremely crowded conditions and give them the cheapest feeds possible. To prevent the spread of disease, the chickens are given high amounts of antibiotics and growth hormones, and treated with bleach after slaughter. No marketing efforts can convince us that this inexpensive chicken is appetizing or healthy for us.

Both organic and specialty (sometimes labelled "natural") chickens are free of antibiotics or growth hormones. Organic chickens must be given an organic feed that isn't genetically modified, must be raised cage free and must have daily access to the outdoors. There is also a legal limit on how many chickens a farmer can raise per square foot of farm. Some specialty chickens are also raised cage free and have outdoor access (check their labels or company websites), but they will not have been given organic feed.

When we made the decision to sell only organic or specialty chicken at our restaurants, Vikram put a local, organic Red Bro breed on Rangoli's menu at a very low price to introduce it to our customers. When the birds, which were new to British Columbia, were delivered to the restaurant that first day, one of our kitchen cooks called to tell us that something was wrong with them—the meat was too pink, the fat was too yellow, and they smelled "too strong." She was impressed when we explained the benefits of Red Bro, as she had not realized the chicken she regularly bought for her children at the supermarket was anything different. Likewise, our front-of-house manager, Akiko, was proud to offer guests this premium meat, so she was visibly upset when a customer wanted to return the chicken dish because it tasted "too chickeny." She tried to explain the quality of the meat, but the customer was insistent that it didn't taste right, and Akiko ended up taking back the dish and throwing it in the garbage. For us, "too chickeny" is exactly how chicken should taste.

Since our daughters love chicken, we make sure to feed them organic, free-range birds. Many people perceive specialty and organic chickens as being expensive, but in this case we disagree. In fact, regular, factory chickens are dangerously cheap. Organic produce, sustainable seafood and organic or specialty poultry and meats do add up, and you may need to reassess your food budget and where your money is being spent. If you are unable to introduce such foods all at once but you and your family do eat meat, we strongly urge you to start by buying organic poultry. You will pay more at the till, but the payoff in terms of the flavour and your long-term health will be worth it.

Dates and Bitter Melon Two Ways:
Vegetarian or with Chicken

BITTER melon (page 66), also called bitter gourd, is highly regarded in India for its health benefits and is known for purifying the blood and helping to reduce blood sugar levels. Its bitterness is an acquired taste for non-Indians, but many Indians love to spice it up and enjoy its punch on the palate. In northern India we marinate it in salt to soften the flavour a bit and then cook bitter melon with lots of strong spices. Here we use bitter melon almost as the main spice in this dish rather than as its main ingredient. We combine it with the sweetness of dates, on a canvas of potatoes in one recipe, on chicken in another.

In North America we use frozen pieces of bitter melon to make this recipe. Several Indian brands are available at most Asian stores in the U.S. and Canada, but just don't confuse the Chinese-style bitter melons with the Indian type. The Chinese bitter melons are big and shiny green, whereas the Indian ones are smaller, darker green and not shiny at all. Indian bitter melons are much stronger in taste. Chop the other vegetables while the bitter melon is thawing.

We find that dates are moister when you buy them whole with the pits in them and then remove the pits by hand at home. Like tomatoes with no juice, extra-dry dates have much less flavour (and are extremely sweet) and serve little purpose in a curry. For best results, use the full quantity of cooking oil recommended here, or you will end up burning either the onions or the spices.

Serve this curry hot with any bread, naan or chapatti and a side dish of yogurt. It also makes a great filling for a sandwich in a bun!

Empty the package of bitter melon into a colander. Run cold water over bitter melon for 30 seconds to speed up the thawing process, then allow it to thaw in the sink.

continued overleaf...

SERVES 6

PREP & COOKING TIME
45 minutes + 30 minutes
to thaw the bitter melon

11 oz package frozen
bitter melon pieces

½ cup cooking oil

1 large onion, sliced

½ tsp asafoetida (optional)

1½ tsp fennel seeds

2 to 3 medium tomatoes, sliced

1 tsp turmeric

1 tsp ground cayenne pepper

1 tsp garam masala (page 41)

1½ lbs potatoes, unpeeled, or
skinless and boneless chicken
breast or chicken thigh, sliced

1 large green or red bell pepper,
seeded and thinly sliced

12 fresh or dried dates,
pitted and roughly chopped

1 Tbsp finely chopped
celery leaves (optional)

SERVE WITH

Roasted Eggplant Raita

Spinach and Split Pea Mash

Paneer, Green Beans
and Eggplant in Tamarind
Curry (for dinner parties)

Preheat the oven to 350°F. Drain bitter melon and gently squeeze out any extra water using your hands. Sift through the pieces and discard any large, tough seeds. Spread bitter melon in a single layer on a baking sheet and bake for 20 minutes. Bitter melon should be slightly shrivelled and dried up (the pieces will still be a bit moist but noticeably shrivelled). If they are not, then bake for another 5 minutes. Remove from the oven and set aside to cool. Once they have cooled, chop bitter melon rounds into smaller, crumb-like pieces.

In a medium pot, heat oil on medium-high for 1 minute. Add onion, stir immediately, then sauté without stirring for 2 to 3 minutes. The edges of the onions should be brown (if not, cook them without stirring for 1 minute more). Stir in asafoetida and fennel seeds and cook for 2 minutes, stirring once. Add bitter melon, tomatoes, turmeric, cayenne and garam masala and stir and sauté for 2 minutes. Stir in potatoes (or chicken), cover and cook for 10 to 12 minutes, or until potatoes are soft but not mushy when pierced with a knife (or juices run clear when chicken is poked with a knife). Stir in bell pepper, dates and celery leaves, cover and turn off the heat. Allow the mixture to steam for 5 minutes. Stir and serve immediately.

Green Cabbage, Peas and Chicken Curry
on Brown Basmati Rice

THIS dish is sort of an Indian version of chicken fried rice but made with brown rice. If you don't eat chicken, you can use extra-firm tofu or tempeh instead, or just make the recipe with extra cabbage and peas. Try not to overcook the cabbage or peas, as they will release water and wilt, and if you are going to use garam masala, use only one tablespoon of cumin. Vikram and Meeru love the onions in this dish, so we just make the girls pick them out rather than not including the full amount of onions. The actual chicken, cabbage, pea curry takes about twenty minutes to prepare, so put the rice on the stove first.

Our girls prefer brown rice over white in this dish because it soaks up the spices better. We don't stir the rice into the chicken before we serve it because we prefer to leave the ratio of rice to chicken up to each person. Nanaki, for example, prefers more rice, whereas Shanik prefers more chicken and vegetables. So, set out a pot of chicken and vegetables and a pot of rice on the dining table, then allow each person to dig in and make his or her own personal pilaf.

Heat oil in a large, heavy-bottomed, shallow pan for 30 seconds on medium-high. Gently stir in tomatoes (or tomato sauce), turmeric, cumin, salt and any or all of coriander, garam masala, paprika, and black pepper (or cayenne) and sauté for 3 to 4 minutes. When oil glistens on top you will know the spices are cooked.

Add chicken strips and onion and stir well. Reduce the heat to medium, cover and cook for 10 to 12 minutes. Uncover the pot, add cabbage, stir well and sauté for 5 minutes, or until slightly crunchy. Check that chicken is cooked by poking it with a knife; the meat should be white with no traces of pink. Stir in peas, then turn off the heat and stir in cilantro.

SERVES 6 TO 8

PREP & COOKING TIME
1 hour (including time to cook the brown rice)

⅓ cup cooking oil

1 small tomato, finely chopped, or 2 Tbsp plain, canned tomato sauce

1 tsp turmeric

1½ Tbsp ground cumin

2 tsp salt

1 Tbsp ground coriander (optional)

1 tsp garam masala (page 41, optional)

1 tsp paprika (optional)

1 tsp black pepper or ground cayenne pepper (optional)

1½ lbs skinless and boneless chicken thighs or breasts, cut in 1-inch x 2-inch strips

1 large red onion, roughly chopped (optional)

½ head of green cabbage (about 1 lb), chopped

12 oz frozen peas, thawed

½ cup chopped cilantro

½ recipe cooked brown basmati rice (page 55)

SERVE WITH

Roasted Eggplant Raita

Spiced Pistachios and Dates

Curried Devilled Eggs

Yam and Tomato Curry

Chicken, Tomato and Green Bean Curry

SERVES 6 TO 8

PREP & COOKING TIME
45 minutes

½ cup cooking oil

2 cups chopped
red onion (1 large)

2 Tbsp chopped garlic
(6 medium cloves)

3 cups chopped
tomatoes (6 medium)

1 tsp turmeric

1½ Tbsp ground cumin

1½ Tbsp mild
Mexican chili powder

1 Tbsp salt

1 tsp ground cayenne
pepper (optional)

2½ lbs skinless and
boneless chicken thighs,
cut in 1-inch strips

½ cup water

1 lb green beans,
trimmed and cut in
½- to 1-inch pieces

SERVE WITH

Tangy and Spicy
Chopped New Potatoes

Brown Basmati and
Portobello Mushroom Pilaf

Mushroom and Celery
Root Basmati Rice Pilaf

WE cook mostly with chicken thighs at home because the organic thighs are cheaper and way juicier than the breast meat. Although this recipe calls for boneless thigh meat, you can just as easily use bone-in thigh (just make sure it's enough meat for six servings and add an extra cup of water so that you can get a nice chicken broth in your curry).

We add fresh green beans for their flavour, colour and nutritional value, but you can use frozen beans if you're pressed for time. Remember, too, that the juicier and sweeter the tomato, the more flavour this curry will have. Serve this dish with rice, couscous, pita bread, naan or even boiled potatoes.

In a large, heavy-bottomed pan, heat oil on medium-high for 1 minute. Add onion and sauté for about 8 minutes, or until light golden on the edges. (Don't overcook the red onion, as it is meant to give a sweeter taste to this curry.) Add garlic and sauté for 2 to 3 minutes, then add tomatoes and stir well. Add turmeric, cumin, chili powder, salt and cayenne and sauté for 5 minutes. Stir in chicken, pour in water and bring to a boil. Reduce the heat to medium, cover and cook for 10 minutes. Remove the lid carefully and stir in green beans. Cook, uncovered, for 5 minutes, or until beans are just slightly crunchy and chicken is cooked (juices run clear when it is poked with a knife).

Oven-baked Chicken and Potatoes
in Yogurt and Date Curry

SERVES 6 TO 8

PREP & BAKING TIME
35 minutes + 45 minutes to bake

12 fresh or dried dates or
8 dried prunes, pitted
+ 1 cup boiling water OR
1½ Tbsp tamarind paste
(page 42) + 1 cup hot water

2 ½ lbs skinless
chicken breast or thigh

2 cups plain, full-fat yogurt
warmed to room
temperature and stirred

⅓ cup cooking oil

1 Tbsp salt

1 tsp ground cayenne pepper

1 Tbsp + 1 tsp garam masala
(page 41) OR 1 Tbsp
ground cumin + 2-inch
cinnamon stick + 5 cloves

1 Tbsp paprika

1 lb new potatoes,
unpeeled and halved,
or 1 lb celery root,
peeled and cut in 2-inch
dice (optional)

THIS chicken dish is slightly tangy, slightly sweet and very succulent. It is also very versatile. We make a one-pot meal by chopping new potatoes in half (with the skins on) and allowing them to cook into the curry. If you prefer the flavour of celery, substitute celery root for the potatoes. Remember that celery root has a very thick skin, so buy a pound and a half of the unpeeled vegetable to obtain enough for this recipe. If you don't wish to add potatoes or celery root, just cook some rice to serve on the side and soak up the curry. If you don't have garam masala, use a combination of ground cumin and either cinnamon or cloves (or both). Although the dish won't have all the spices, you'll still get an additional layer of flavour. You can also substitute dried prunes or tamarind paste for the dates.

We prefer chicken thigh meat for this recipe, but the yogurt will keep breast meat tender as well. Some friends who are avid cooks have made this curry, and the yogurt has curdled during the baking process. We haven't had this issue as long as we use full-fat yogurt and temper it with hot water. Basically, you don't want cold yogurt to go into a very hot oven. If you'd rather not use yogurt, you can use stirred coconut milk instead. However, we prefer the taste of the yogurt.

You can use any cut of chicken you wish, and you can bake it either bone-in or boneless. Bone-in will give the dish added flavour. If you use breast meat, watch the cooking time closely so that it does not overcook. You could just as easily substitute stewing beef or stewing lamb for the chicken, but increase the baking time to at least 1 hour and up to 1½ hours. Although the baking time may vary slightly from oven to oven, the heavier the baking dish you use, the more succulent the chicken or other meat will be.

Preheat the oven to 350°F.

In a small bowl, combine dates (or prunes) and boiling water and stir well. Soak for 5 minutes, then strain through a sieve, using the back of a spoon to push as much of the fruit as possible through the sieve. You will have a date (or prune) "juice." Discard any solids left in the sieve. (If you are using tamarind paste, you don't need to add boiling water or strain it; just mix it with hot tap water.)

In a large bowl, combine chicken, yogurt, date juice (or prune juice or tamarind juice), oil, salt, cayenne, garam masala (or cumin and cinnamon and cloves), paprika and potatoes (or celery root). Transfer the mixture to a heavy baking dish, cover with a lid and bake for 40 to 45 minutes, or until chicken is cooked (juices run clear when it is poked with a knife). Serve immediately.

SERVE WITH

Quinoa Salad with Lentil Sprouts

Turnips and Tomatoes in Kalonji Masala

Spicy Cauliflower "Steak"

Butter Chicken Schnitzel

Homestyle butter sauce

¼ cup cooking oil

2 to 3 Tbsp crushed garlic
(6 to 9 medium cloves)

1 small can tomato
paste or ¾ cup crushed
canned tomatoes

1 Tbsp paprika

1 tsp turmeric

1½ tsp salt

1 tsp ground cumin
(or 1 Tbsp if you are
not using garam masala)

2 tsp garam masala
(page 41, optional)

1 tsp ground coriander (optional)

1 tsp ground cayenne
pepper (optional)

1½ cups water

1½ cups whipping cream

YOU will never see this recipe on one of our restaurant menus, but it is a regular indulgence at our house. It is a rich dish combining "butter sauce" and chicken nuggets that Vikram created for Nanaki and Shanik.

The inspiration came at a local restaurant one night, when the girls were whining for the chicken nuggets from the kids' menu. Meeru was trying to get them to try something else and getting increasingly irritated at their refusal. The next evening Vikram decided to show the girls what "real" chicken nuggets are—chicken schnitzel. He taught them each step, and at some point Nanaki joked, "Hey, let's make butter chicken schnitzel!" Seizing the opportunity to get her to cook and eat Indian food, Vikram made this sauce on the spot. Nanaki and Shanik were thrilled, and this is now our signature family dish. The girls also quit ordering chicken nuggets at restaurants.

Before he even owned a restaurant, Vikram had vowed that he would never serve butter chicken. We have stuck to that vow in our fifteen years, if for no other reason than there are plenty of restaurants already serving it. It also keeps us creative. For this recipe we use boneless organic chicken thighs when they're available or boneless organic breast meat when they are not. We also prepare our own quick homestyle butter sauce rather than a restaurant-style version. Since there are plenty of chicken (or pork) schnitzel recipes, feel free to use your favourite recipe if you already have one. It is the combination we are sharing with you.

We've written this recipe for six medium portions, but add more chicken if you wish, since you will have more than enough flour, egg and bread crumbs. You can always reheat the chicken in the oven the next day. We recommend that you use a garlic crusher to make this dish, as the sauce is supposed to be very creamy and garlicky. If you like garlic, use the larger amount. You will need to clear some counter space for making this meal.

When it's just the four of us, we serve the chicken like a fondue, with the sauce in one big bowl in the middle of the table. If you prefer, pour the sauce into individual dipping bowls and have each guest dip away.

Homestyle butter sauce Heat oil in a medium pot on medium for 1 minute. Add garlic and sauté for 1 minute, or until golden. It will become slightly sticky, but keep stirring. Add tomato paste (or crushed tomatoes)

and stir well, then reduce the heat to low and add paprika, turmeric, salt, cumin, garam masala, coriander and cayenne. Stir well and sauté for 4 minutes. Stir in water and cream, then turn off the heat and set aside until you are ready to serve.

Chicken schnitzel Place the pieces of chicken on a counter top and lightly pound them with the heel of your hand. Set chicken aside on a plate.

Spread flour on another plate and mix in salt. Spread bread crumbs on a third plate. Beat the eggs in a large bowl. Line a baking sheet with paper towels.

Dip a piece of chicken in the flour to lightly coat both sides. Shake off any excess flour, then dip the chicken into the beaten eggs to lightly coat both sides. Finally, dredge the chicken in the bread crumbs, making sure to coat both sides and shake off any excess. Place the coated chicken pieces on an unlined baking sheet. Repeat with the remaining chicken pieces.

continued overleaf...

Chicken schnitzel

2 lbs boneless chicken breasts or thighs, cut in 2-inch x 3-inch pieces

½ cup all-purpose flour

1 tsp salt

1 cup fine bread crumbs

2 eggs

½ to ¾ cup cooking oil

SERVE WITH

Tomato and Onion
Chutney (as a replacement for
the homestyle butter sauce)

Beet Greens Sautéed
in Ginger, Lemon and Cumin

Quinoa Salad with Lentil Sprouts

Heat 2 Tbsp of the oil in a deep-sided frying pan on medium-high for 3 to 4 minutes, or until oil is hot enough that chicken will start to cook immediately. (If the oil isn't hot enough, it will soak into the bread crumbs and you will have greasy rather than crispy chicken.) Use a pair of tongs to add each piece of chicken (as many as will easily fit in your pan), then pan-fry each side for 3 minutes. Use a knife to cut into the first cooked piece: the meat should be white without any pink, and the flesh should be succulent, not dry. (If bread crumbs begin to burn within 1 minute, then reduce the heat. If oil is not sizzling around the chicken, increase the heat.) Transfer the cooked chicken schnitzel to the lined baking sheet to drain. Repeat with the remaining pieces of chicken.

Finish butter sauce Once all (or most) of the chicken has been fried, warm the sauce on medium-high heat. As soon as it boils, stir well and reduce the heat to low. Simmer for 5 minutes, then turn off the heat.

Coconut Curried Chicken

NDIAN cooking lends itself to darker chicken meat, as lean white meat is easy to overcook. If you wish to use chicken breast for this curry, be careful not to allow it to become dry. Whichever cut you use, buy it with the bone in to create a stock for the curry. Once the chicken is cooked, remove the bones and serve the chicken curry without them.

Curry leaves are available at most Indian grocers, but be sure to buy green ones, as the brownish-tinged ones are on the verge of going bad and have little to no flavour. We prefer puréed onion, which adds a rich, velvety texture and a deeper flavour to the curry; however, if you are pressed for time or want to use less oil, finely chop the onion and sauté it quickly in a third of a cup of oil. Serve with rice or naan.

Heat oil in a large, heavy-bottomed pot on medium-high for 1 minute. Add cumin seeds and allow them to sizzle for 30 seconds (or add mustard seeds and allow them to sizzle until you hear the first popping sounds). Add cayenne and stir in onion. Sauté onion for 10 to 12 minutes, stirring regularly. A little of the onion will to stick to the pot, giving the curry a stronger onion flavour. If onion is becoming dark brown and burning, reduce the heat.

When onion is very light brown, add garlic, stir and sauté for another 3 to 4 minutes, or until golden. Reduce the heat to medium, add ginger and sauté for 1 to 2 minutes. Stir in tomato, then add turmeric, curry leaves, salt and cloves. Stir and cook for 5 minutes, or until oil glistens on the tomatoes. Turn off the heat and stir in chicken, then coconut milk. Turn the heat to high and bring to a boil. Reduce the heat to medium, cover and cook for 30 minutes, or until chicken is cooked. To check for doneness, cut into a piece of chicken with a sharp knife and make sure there is no pink meat. Turn off the heat and allow to cool for 30 minutes if you are serving the chicken boneless.

To serve boneless, using a large ladle, carefully transfer chicken to a large bowl, leaving the coconut curry in the pot. Wearing plastic gloves, peel the meat from the bones. Discard the bones, and return the chicken meat to the curry. Stir well to combine. At this point, you may wish to take out some or most of the curry leaves, as they are difficult to chew.

Just before serving, bring the curry to a boil on medium-high heat. Turn off the heat and stir in cilantro.

SERVES 6

PREP & COOKING TIME
50 minutes

½ cup cooking oil

1½ tsp cumin seeds
or black mustard seeds

3 large or 6 medium dried
cayenne peppers, cut in
halves or quarters (optional)

1 cup puréed onion (1 large)

3½ Tbsp finely chopped
garlic (10 to 11 medium cloves)

1½ Tbsp finely chopped ginger

¾ cup puréed tomato (1 large)

½ tsp turmeric

20 fresh curry leaves (optional)

1 Tbsp salt

10 cloves

3 lbs skinless chicken
thighs, bones in

4 cups coconut milk, stirred

½ cup chopped cilantro (optional)

SERVE WITH

Tomato and Onion Chutney

Red Bell Pepper
and Shallot Curry

Eggplant and Navy Beans
in Kalonji and Tamarind Curry
(for dinner parties)

Chicken with Crimini Mushrooms
and Saffron Curry

SERVES 6 TO 8

PREP & COOKING TIME
1½ hours

½ cup cooking oil

2½ lbs red onions,
chopped (2 very large)

6 to 7 Tbsp chopped garlic
(18 to 21 medium cloves!)

1 Tbsp salt

½ tsp turmeric

½ Tbsp ground cayenne pepper

2 Tbsp paprika (optional)

3½ lbs skinless chicken
thighs, bones in

4 cups water

4 cups whipping cream

8 oz crimini mushrooms, sliced

1 Tbsp dried green
fenugreek leaves

¼ tsp saffron
(about 20 threads)
in ¼ cup hot water

SERVE WITH

Spinach and Split Pea Mash

Tangy and Spicy
Chopped New Potatoes

Chickpeas in Star Anise and
Date Masala (for dinner parties)

Cook the chicken in this curry with the bones in, along with lots of garlic and onions. We've suggested a moderate amount of saffron, but add more or less, depending on the quality of the spice. When we use lovely deep orange–red saffron, we only need about ten threads. Good-quality saffron is very expensive, but it's worth the price and keeps fresh for about a month when stored in an airtight container.

This is a very rich curry but it's not heavily spiced, so it's another of the many curries that children enjoy. On days when the kids have no school, Meeru sometimes brings Shanik and her friends to Vij's, and when this curry is on the menu the girls always eat it for lunch. Serve this curry over rice, or with naan, slices of baguette or another hearty bread that will soak up the masala.

Heat oil in a medium pot on medium-high for 1 minute. Add onions and sauté for 6 to 8 minutes, until edges are lightly browned. Reduce the heat to medium, add garlic and sauté for 5 to 6 minutes, or until light brown. Stir in salt, turmeric, cayenne and paprika and sauté for 1 more minute. Add chicken and cook, stirring regularly, for 5 minutes. Stir in water and cream, increase the heat to medium-high and bring to a boil. Reduce the heat to low, cover and simmer for 25 to 30 minutes. To check for doneness, cut into a piece of chicken with a sharp knife to make sure there is no pink meat. Turn off the heat and allow the curry to cool for at least 30 minutes, or until chicken is cool enough to handle.

Wearing plastic gloves, peel the meat from the bones. Discard the bones, and return the chicken meat to the curry. Stir in mushrooms.

Just before serving, bring the curry to a light boil on medium heat. Stir in fenugreek plus saffron and its soaking water. Turn off the heat and serve.

Chicken Breast and Thighs
in Clove, Black Cardamom and Yogurt Curry

PREP & COOKING TIME
3 hours to marinate +
20 minutes to grill chicken
breast; 1 hour to braise
chicken thighs

Chicken breast

1½ lbs skinless and boneless chicken breast, trimmed of fat

⅓ cup cooking oil

1 Tbsp salt

1 Tbsp ground cumin

1 Tbsp ground coriander

1 tsp ground cayenne pepper (optional)

1 Tbsp paprika (optional)

1 tsp ground dried ginger (optional)

IN this recipe we cook the same ingredients two separate ways and then serve them together. We oven-braise the chicken thighs, as the darker meat is much juicier and soaks in the spices while lending its flavour to the broth. We marinate and then grill the chicken breast, as this is the best way to retain the succulence of the white meat. Feel free to make just one of these recipes and serve it on its own: the chicken breast may be a better warm-weather recipe, since you can easily grill it on the barbecue.

Black cardamom is available at any Indian grocer. While you're there, look for dried ground ginger (known as *soond*) whose stronger flavour we prefer to fresh ginger in this recipe. If you use *soond*, make sure to break any clumps into a powder.

Since this is a very robust curry, we always serve it with Indian white basmati rice (page 56) in a large bowl. At Vij's we also serve it with Red Bell Pepper and Shallot Curry (page 87).

Chicken breast In a medium bowl, combine chicken breasts with oil, salt, cumin, coriander, cayenne, paprika and ginger. (Do not use fresh ginger, as it burns while you grill the chicken.) Toss lightly to coat the chicken, then cover and refrigerate for at least 3 hours.

Chicken thighs Preheat the oven to 350°F.

With a knife, lightly crack the cardamom pods. With your fingers, peel back the shell to release the black seeds and collect them in a small bowl. (The best seeds are dark and stuck together. If they are light brown and dry, they won't have much flavour, so discard them and crush a few more pods to get enough fresh seeds.) Discard the shells. With a rolling pin or a mortar and pestle, crush the cardamom seeds (or leave them whole if you don't mind biting into them). Set aside.

In a medium cassoulet dish (or another baking dish with a lid), combine chicken thighs, cardamom seeds, yogurt, tomatoes, garlic, oil, salt, cayenne, coriander, cumin, paprika, ginger, celery seed, cloves and water. Mix well, cover and bake for about 40 to 45 minutes, or until chicken is cooked through. To test for doneness, cut into chicken with a sharp knife to be sure there is no pink meat.

Remove chicken from the oven, but keep covered until you are ready to serve, as doing so keeps the chicken curry warm.

Finish chicken breasts Once the chicken thighs have been in the oven for 35 minutes, preheat the barbecue or stovetop iron grill to high.

Place marinated chicken breasts on the grill and cook for 4 to 5 minutes. Turn chicken over and grill for another 4 to 5 minutes. Gently poke one breast with a knife to check if it's cooked through. If the meat is still pink, grill each side for 1 minute more and check again.

Chicken thighs

3 to 4 black cardamom pods (optional)

1½ lbs skinless and boneless chicken thighs, trimmed of fat

1½ cups plain yogurt (minimum 2% milk fat), stirred

1½ cups puréed tomatoes (2 to 3 medium)

3 Tbsp finely chopped garlic (9 medium cloves)

¼ cup cooking oil

1 Tbsp + 1 tsp salt

½ Tbsp ground cayenne pepper (optional)

2 Tbsp ground coriander

3 Tbsp ground cumin

1 Tbsp + 1 tsp paprika (optional)

1 tsp ground dried ginger or 2 ½ Tbsp finely chopped fresh ginger (optional)

1 Tbsp celery seed

10 cloves (optional)

1 cup water

SERVE WITH

Celery, Tomato and Green Onion Sauté

Celery and Navy Bean Salad

Red Bell Pepper and Shallot Curry

Marinated Duck Breast
with Mung Bean and Sesame Seed Rice Pilaf

ALTHOUGH we combine this pilaf with duck breast, on its own it is a delight for vegetarians as well. Although the richness of the pilaf is perfect with gamier poultry such as duck, you can also serve it with any meat, fish or vegetable curry in this book. In combination with duck, we usually serve it with either the Coconut Curry for Any Day and Any Dish (page 77) or the Ground Fennel Seed Curry (page 78). Either heap the rice on a large platter and arrange the duck pieces around it, or spoon the pilaf onto individual plates or large shallow bowls along with five to six pieces of duck per serving. Top each portion of pilaf (and duck) with piping hot curry.

Indian nutritional wisdom emphasizes nuts (almonds, cashews and pine nuts) and seeds (such as sesame, sunflower, pumpkin and even melon). Nanaki is severely allergic to peanuts and pine nuts—and witnessing a severe allergic reaction can turn you off serving any type of nuts to your child. Sesame seeds are a perfect replacement for nuts in Nanaki's diet and are, arguably, healthier per serving. They are high in calcium, manganese, copper, thiamine and iron, among other nutrients. Roasted sesame seeds add a subtle, nutty flavour that comes as a pleasant surprise in an Indian pilaf. However, sesame seeds can be optional if you really don't like their taste or are allergic to them.

Mung beans begin to pop once they are cooked. The longer they cook, the more they pop and become mushy, which is fine for a curry or soup but not for a rice pilaf. Therefore, in this recipe watch carefully and try to turn off the heat just before the beans pop, which will ensure they don't overcook or lose their shape and texture. Check them often during the last ten minutes of cooking.

Finally, this dish involves lots of pots and pans, so factor in an extra ten minutes of clean-up in addition to your cooking time. Although preparing this dish takes many steps, this isn't a difficult recipe, especially after you've made it once and gain a better handle on cooking times for the mung beans and duck breast. If you prefer more rice or more lentils, you can play around with the measurements as long as the total measurement for both is 2 cups. The pilaf on its own is quite simple to prepare.

continued overleaf...

SERVES 6

PREP & COOKING TIME
8 to 24 hours to marinate
+ 30 minutes to cook duck;
45 minutes to make pilaf

Marinated duck breasts

3 duck breasts
(1 lb each), skin on

½ cup cooking oil

1 Tbsp ground cumin

1 tsp salt

1 tsp ground cayenne pepper

1 tsp ground fenugreek
seeds (optional)

1 tsp ground black
mustard seeds (optional)

1 tsp garam masala
(page 41, optional)

Mung bean and sesame pilaf

1 cup white basmati rice

5 ¾ cups water

1 tsp butter

2 tsp salt

1 cup mung beans

4 Tbsp sesame seeds

⅓ cup cooking oil

2 Tbsp finely chopped
garlic (6 medium cloves)

2 bunches green onions, whites
and green parts, finely chopped

2 Tbsp finely chopped ginger

½ tsp turmeric

1 tsp crushed cayenne
pepper (optional)

Marinated duck breasts Cut each duck breast in half lengthwise to create six servings. In a large bowl, combine duck with oil, cumin, salt, cayenne, fenugreek seeds, mustard seeds and garam masala. Mix well, cover and refrigerate for 8 to 10 hours. (If you want to begin the duck the night before, you can marinate it for almost 24 hours before cooking.)

Mung bean and sesame pilaf Place rice in a medium pot, wash it well under cold water and drain. Repeat the washing and draining once more. Add 1¾ cups of the water, butter and 1 tsp of the salt in a medium pot and soak for 20 minutes. Bring to a boil on high heat, then reduce the heat to low, cover and simmer for 12 minutes. Turn off the heat and allow to sit, covered, for 8 to 10 minutes. Remove the lid and stir with a fork to ensure rice is flaky. Set aside.

While rice is soaking, place mung beans in a medium pot, wash them well under cold water and drain. Repeat once more. Add the remaining 4 cups water, then bring to a boil on high heat. Reduce the heat to medium-low, cover and boil for 25 minutes, or until beans are cooked but not mushy. (Taste a bean, and if it is not cooked, put the lid back on the pot and check the beans every 3 minutes until they are ready.) Immediately turn off the heat, drain the beans in a colander and set aside (or, if the rice is cooked, gently pour them into the pot with the rice).

Heat a small frying pan on high for 30 seconds. Reduce the heat to medium-high and gently pour in sesame seeds. Stir constantly with a wooden spoon for 1 to 2 minutes, or until sesame seeds have become a shade (or two) darker, but not brown. Turn off the heat and transfer sesame seeds to a bowl to cool.

Heat oil in another frying pan on medium-high for 1 minute. Add garlic and sauté for 3 to 4 minutes, or until light brown. Add green onions and sauté for 3 to 4 minutes, or until shrivelled and a bit crispy. Stir in ginger and sauté for 1 minute. Add turmeric, the remaining 1 tsp of salt and cayenne, then stir, sauté for 2 minutes and turn off the heat.

To the rice, add mung beans (if you have not already), roasted sesame seeds and sautéed spices. Stir gently, but thoroughly, with a fork. Serve immediately or set aside while you prepare the duck breasts.

Finish duck Preheat the oven to 375°F.

Heat an ovenproof frying pan on high for 1 minute. Keeping your head away from the pan, carefully place 1 or 2 duck breasts, skin side down, in the pan (do not squeeze them in since you need to turn them over). The fat of the duck skin will sizzle loudly as it touches the hot pan. Sear duck for 2 minutes, then turn over and sear for another 2 minutes. Transfer to a plate and sear the remaining duck breasts.

Once all the duck has been seared, place as many pieces as you can in the frying pan and bake for 8 minutes, or until light pink in the middle (check by gently poking with a knife). Remove from the oven and arrange cooked duck breasts in a single layer on a clean cutting board. Bake the remaining duck breasts, then transfer them to the cutting board. Allow cooked duck to rest at room temperature for at least 5 to 10 minutes, or up to 30 minutes. Cut each duck breast into 5 or 6 rounds before serving.

SERVE WITH

Oven-baked Spicy Brussels Sprouts Crumble and Sour Cream Curry

Rapini and Shiitake Mushroom Curry (without the duck, for a vegetarian meal)

Steamed Sablefish OR Steamed Marinated Halibut (instead of the duck) and Ground Fennel Seed Curry

MEATS

WESTERN CUTS OF meat have only recently been introduced to Indian cuisine, and attitudes towards meat are changing quickly in India. Ten years ago, it would have been unheard of to write about beef, but now urban journalists publish stories about its various cuts and quality. In particular, we recently read an article in New Delhi about the virtues of Irish beef, which encouraged readers to try out steak.

In Vancouver, if we want to serve the best of what is available, we can't ignore beef and pork tenderloin, rack of lamb and beef short ribs, to name a few. Indian curries are a natural, if not traditional, fit for these cuts; they cook quickly, and as long as you don't overcook the meats, they are very tender. Medium-rare is common in North America, but pink meat is less popular in India.

Naturally, tender cuts of meat are expensive, so they are more for special occasions. Likewise, it makes no sense to kill a cow, pig or lamb just for the tenderloin, and many Indian recipes take advantage of the numerous benefits of other cuts. In general, stewing cuts are less expensive, so you can buy organic or natural meats, and they are reasonably priced for what you get. Stewing cuts are generally from the legs of the animal, including the meaty upper leg portion. Although the leg meat is not as toothsome as the more premium cuts, the meat is very tender and full of flavor once you have cooked it long enough.

Stewing takes longer than some other types of cooking, but it can be done in the oven, on a stovetop or in a pressure cooker. Typically, you add liquid to the meat and cook it over low temperature for one to two hours. Or, you add liquid to the meat and cook it in the pressure cooker for about ten minutes. As the meat cooks, it releases its own juices, making for a rich and delicious broth that keeps the dish moist. Unlike more expensive cuts, stewed meats, therefore, are difficult to overcook. Stewed curries are easy to reheat and taste even better the next day.

When cooking or reheating stewed meats, just make sure to use a pot with a tight-fitting lid and add enough liquid to create steam.

Lamb in Creamy Green Cardamom Curry

SERVES 6 TO 8

PREP & COOKING TIME
30 minutes + 1 hour to stew on the stove; 15 minutes + 1 to 1½ hours to cook in the oven

⅓ to ½ cup cooking oil

2 cups chopped onion (1 large)

½ tsp asafoetida (optional)

4 Tbsp chopped garlic (12 medium cloves)

¾ cup crushed canned tomatoes

1½ tsp turmeric

1½ Tbsp ground black mustard seeds (optional)

1½ tsp ground cayenne pepper (optional)

1 Tbsp paprika

2 Tbsp ground cumin

10 to 12 green cardamom pods, lightly pounded

1 Tbsp salt

3 lbs stewing lamb, trimmed of fat and cubed

1 cup water (for oven method) or 2 cups water (for stovetop method)

1½ cups buttermilk or plain, full-fat yogurt, warmed to room temperature and stirred OR ¾ cup whipping cream

THERE are two main ways to make this dish. For dinner parties, we cook the traditional way on the stovetop, sautéing the onions and masala in a pot and then cooking the lamb. But on workdays, Meeru mixes all the ingredients together in a large casserole dish and puts everything in the oven about 1½ hours before dinner. The oven method doesn't have the same punch or deep colour of the sautéed masala, but when convenience reigns, it's still delicious. Nanaki prefers the oven method, as the spices aren't as strong.

Often, Nanaki and Shanik do the mixing. For them, it's like playing with playdough. They don't like to wear gloves, so their hands and the counter do get messy. Nevertheless, if they've had anything to do with making the meal, it automatically tastes good to them. You can leave the curry in the oven once you turn it off, as the lamb only gets more tender.

Feel free to replace the buttermilk with either stirred yogurt or whipping cream. Buttermilk or yogurt gives the curry a slight tang, whereas the cream makes it richer. We serve this lamb curry with rice or naan bread, but it is also delicious over boiled, salted potatoes.

For the oven method, move your oven rack to the middle position and preheat the oven to 375°F.

Place all ingredients in a large casserole dish and mix until well combined. Cover with a lid or aluminum foil, place in the oven and bake for 1 hour. Using a sharp knife, poke a piece of lamb to make sure it is tender. If it is still slightly tough in the centre, bake for another 15 to 30 minutes, or until cooked. Turn off the heat and allow lamb to rest in the oven, covered, until serving time.

For the stovetop method, heat oil in a large, heavy-bottomed pan on high for 1 minute. Add onion and sauté for 5 to 6 minutes, or until golden. Add asafoetida and stir for 1 minute. Stir in garlic and sauté until golden, 1 to 2 minutes. Reduce the heat to medium and stir in tomatoes. Add turmeric, mustard seeds, cayenne, paprika, cumin, cardamom and salt, stir and cook for 5 minutes, or until oil glistens on the tomatoes.

Stir in lamb, mixing until well combined. Pour in water and mix well. Increase the heat to high and bring to a boil, then reduce the heat to medium-low, cover and cook for 50 minutes.

Place buttermilk (or yogurt or cream) in a medium bowl. To prevent curdling, whisk about 1 cup of the hot curry into the buttermilk (or yogurt or cream), then pour the mixture into the pot of curry. Cover and continue cooking for 15 minutes. Using a sharp knife, poke a piece of lamb to make sure it is tender. If it is still slightly tough in the centre, continue cooking for another 15 minutes, or until tender. (It has never taken us longer than 1½ hours to cook the lamb.) Turn off the heat and allow lamb to rest on the stove, covered, until serving time.

SERVE WITH

Eggplant and Paneer Pâté

Punjabi Lentil Curry

Eggplant and Navy Beans in Kalonji and Tamarind Curry (for dinner parties)

Spice-encrusted Lamb Popsicles

MEERU came up with this recipe for Mike Bernardo, Vij's general manager, to serve at one of his parties. The theme for the evening was red meat and alcohol (no juice or soda on offer), and guests were instructed to "hydrate before you come."

We consider these popsicles to be a glorified, high-end variation on chicken wings. We have our butcher cut each "popsicle" from the rack of lamb so that guests have individual chops to pick up and eat with their hands. That way we can serve this dish as an hors d'oeuvre or part of a larger meal. Once the lamb has marinated, this recipe is fast and easy and tastes great, as long as you don't burn the chops in the oven or marinate the lamb for more than a day (the spices get too intense). Use the recommended amount of oil to cook the spices in the oven, as any less changes the flavour.

Although you can serve these popsicles on their own, they are delicious with the sour cream Indian dressing (page 43) or chutneys (pages 44 to 49) as a dip. We have given a baking time for popsicles with a slightly pink centre; if you prefer them cooked more, adjust the baking time accordingly.

In a large bowl, combine lamb with oil, cumin, salt, cayenne, coriander, paprika, turmeric and garlic. Toss lightly to coat the lamb, then cover and refrigerate for 2 to 3 hours to allow lamb to marinate.

Move your oven rack to its highest position, and preheat the oven to 500°F.

On a large baking sheet, arrange chops—as many as will fit comfortably without overlapping (at home we usually cook 12 to 18 at a time)—and bake for 2 minutes. Remove from the oven (closing the oven door so that the heat doesn't escape), set on a heatproof surface and, using tongs, turn each chop over. Bake for 2 minutes more, then remove from the oven. Using a sharp knife, cut into a popsicle; it should be pink in the centre. (If the popsicles are not quite cooked, bake each side for 30 seconds to 1 minute more.) Transfer to a serving platter and squeeze some lemon juice over the cooked popsicles.

SERVES 6

PREP & COOKING TIME
20 minutes + 2 to 3 hours to marinate the lamb

3½ to 4 lbs rack of lamb, cut into 30 chops

½ cup cooking oil

2 Tbsp ground cumin

1½ tsp salt

1 to 1½ tsp ground cayenne pepper

2 Tbsp ground coriander

1 Tbsp paprika

1 tsp turmeric

2 Tbsp finely chopped garlic (6 medium cloves)

½ to 1 whole lemon, cut in wedges (optional)

SERVE WITH

Apple Chutney

Coconut Curry for Any Day and Any Dish

Coconut Vegetable Curry

Ground Lamb, Beef and Lentil Kebobs

SERVES 10 TO 15
(makes 30 to 35 kebobs)

PREP & COOKING TIME
40 minutes + 15 minutes
to grill or bake

OUR friends Jeremy and Heather came over one Sunday evening to learn how to make kebobs. Heather is mostly vegetarian and saves meat for special occasions, but Jeremy more than compensates for her in the meat-eating department. They were soon to be married, and rather than asking for traditional gifts, they wanted their friends and family to contribute various food items for their wedding dinner. Jeremy had made up a list of foods they needed, then went around coordinating with everyone. We offered to make kebobs.

Although we made several kebob recipes that night at our home, this one below was our favourite and was the one that we made for their wedding. The wedding dinner was a big feast and almost as visually spectacular as the orange polar fleece suit (made from recycled plastic) that Jeremy wore that night.

For this recipe use any ratio of the ground meats you prefer—or even all lamb or all beef. We find that eating low-fat kebobs is like eating a low-fat hamburger or meatballs—not worth it in terms of the loss of taste and succulence. So, buy regular ground meat rather than extra lean for this recipe. We use ground split moong (or mung) lentils instead of bread crumbs, though you can substitute an equal amount of ground bread crumbs for the lentils if you are in a hurry. The lentils add more nutrition and fibre to the kebobs and give them a mildly different flavour. The lentils also go well with the dried mint and green onions. We don't recommend that you try to grind whole mung beans, as they are hard and can break the blades of your spice (or coffee) grinder. Be sure to buy the split green moong lentils, as the split and washed moong lentils, which are yellow, are much too soft when cooked.

Make this entire recipe, and then freeze whatever you don't use for later. The uncooked kebob meat will keep in a resealable plastic bag or in an airtight container for up to 3 months. When you're ready to make them, just thaw the meat and form and bake kebobs according to the recipe below.

Lightly oil a baking sheet and set aside.

In a large bowl, combine lamb (and/or beef), lentils, egg, salt, cayenne, garlic, ginger, green onions, mint and paprika (or sumac) and mix well. Rub a bit of cooking oil on your hands (or on your plastic gloves if you wish to keep your hands clean) and pinch off 1½ to 2 Tbsp of the meat mixture. Roll the meat between your hands to make a log about 3 to 4 inches long and 1 inch in diameter, roughly the size and shape of a medium hot dog. Place the finished kebob on the baking sheet. Repeat with the remaining meat until you have 30 to 35 kebobs. (You will have to keep applying oil to your hands as you make the kebobs.)

To grill the kebobs, preheat a barbecue to high heat. Place kebobs on the grill and cook for 5 minutes, turning often. Kebobs should be well done but not blackened. If they are burning, reduce the heat slightly. Poke the meat with a knife to be sure it's completely cooked; there should be no pink in the centre. Using tongs, remove the cooked kebobs from the grill.

To roast the kebobs in the oven, preheat the oven to 400°F. Place kebobs on a baking sheet, leaving about ¼ inch around each one. Cover with aluminum foil, place in the middle of the oven and bake for 20 minutes. The kebobs will sizzle as they cook. Very carefully remove the foil, keeping your head away from the baking sheet, as hot steam will be released. Serve immediately.

¼ cup cooking oil (for baking sheet and rubbing on hands)

3 lbs ground lamb (or beef, or both)

1 cup ground split moong (green) lentils

1 egg

1½ tsp salt

1 Tbsp crushed cayenne pepper

3 Tbsp finely chopped garlic (9 medium cloves)

2 Tbsp finely chopped ginger

2 cups finely chopped green onions, white and tender green parts

2 Tbsp dried mint

1 Tbsp + 1 tsp paprika or ground sumac (optional)

SERVE WITH

Any of the chutneys in this book

Yam and Tomato Curry

Any of the mushroom recipes in this book

Beef and Broccoli Stew

with Maggi and Soy Sauces

SERVES 10

PREP & COOKING TIME
20 minutes + 1 hour to simmer (or 35 to 40 minutes total in a pressure cooker)

1 to 1¼ cups cooking oil

3 cups chopped onions (2 medium-large)

3 Tbsp finely chopped garlic (9 medium cloves)

2 cups chopped tomatoes (4 medium, but you can used canned, diced)

1 Tbsp chopped ginger

3 Tbsp ground cumin

2 Tbsp ground coriander

1 Tbsp paprika

1 Tbsp ground cayenne pepper (optional)

1 Tbsp salt

3½ lbs lean stewing beef (preferably organic), cut in 1½- to 2-inch dice

2½ cups water

1½ lbs broccoli, cut in 1½-inch pieces

3 Tbsp Maggi sauce (mild or spicy, you can choose)

3 Tbsp soy sauce

½ to ¾ cup chopped cilantro

SERVE WITH

Quinoa Salad with Lentil Sprouts

Celery and Navy Bean Salad

Any of the rice pilafs in this book

THIS simple stew recipe is mostly Indian but has a touch of Chinese because of the soy sauce. Maggi sauce is a spicy masala ketchup that is available from all Indian grocers and some large supermarkets in big cities.

The advantage of cooking with less expensive cuts of meat such as stewing beef is that you can buy it organic at a decent price. Indians like the broccoli stems as much as the florets, so we use both in this recipe. Cooking just the florets is also fine, but don't skimp on the oil, as this recipe involves lots of sautéing.

If you are not feeding a crowd, halve the recipe or cover and refrigerate the leftovers and enjoy this curry for up to a week. Serve it with bowls of rice or pieces of your favourite bread.

Heat ½ cup of the oil in a large heavy-bottomed frying pan on medium-high for 1 minute. Add onions and sauté for 10 minutes, or until golden with some brown edges. (If onions are sticking to the pan and burning, you may need to add another ¼ cup oil.)

Stir in garlic and sauté for another 2 to 3 minutes, or until light brown. Add tomatoes and ginger and stir well. Add cumin, coriander, paprika, cayenne and salt, then stir and sauté this masala for 5 minutes, or until oil glistens on top. Stir in beef cubes and water and bring to a boil. Reduce the heat to low, cover and cook for 1 hour, stirring occasionally.

While the stew is cooking, in a separate frying pan, heat ½ cup of the oil on medium for 1 minute. Add broccoli and sauté, stirring regularly, for 5 minutes, or until cooked to your preferred texture. Set aside.

After an hour, check that beef is cooked by tasting a piece to see if it is tender. Return to the heat, if necessary, to cook it further, or turn off the heat and allow the stew to sit, covered, for 5 minutes. Remove the lid and stir in broccoli, Maggi sauce, soy sauce and cilantro. Serve immediately.

Stewed Beef and Rapini
in Cumin Curry

SERVES 6 TO 8

PREP & COOKING TIME
1 hour and 15 minutes on the stovetop (or 35 minutes in a pressure cooker)

6 oz rapini (without the tough bottom stems), finely chopped

½ cup cooking oil

½ Tbsp cumin seeds

2 cups finely chopped onion (1 large)

2 Tbsp finely chopped garlic (6 medium cloves)

1½ Tbsp finely chopped ginger (optional)

½ tsp asafoetida (optional)

1 Tbsp crushed cayenne pepper (optional)

1 Tbsp ground coriander

1 tsp ajwain seeds (optional)

1 tsp ground cumin

1 Tbsp salt

1 cup puréed tomatoes (2 medium)

2 lbs stewing beef, trimmed of fat and cubed

¾ cup water

SERVE WITH

Spinach and Split Pea Mash

Celery and Navy Bean Salad

Any of the rice pilafs in this book

THIS beef and vegetable stew is made with rapini, which is also known as Italian broccoli and is similar to Chinese gai lan. It has the texture of mustard greens, but has a different, less pungent flavour. The ajwain seeds give the dish a slight oregano or thyme-like flavour. Look for this spice at any Indian grocer, but if you can't find it, make this dish without it. It will just be a simpler curry.

There isn't much liquid in this dish, so we recommend you buy lean beef, as extra-lean beef tends to be drier in texture. And serve this curry with naan or chapatti, or with rice if you prefer.

Place rapini in a colander, wash it and allow it to drain while you make the masala.

Heat oil in a large heavy pot on medium-high for 1 minute. Sprinkle in cumin seeds and allow them to sizzle for 30 seconds. Add onion and sauté for 8 to 10 minutes, or until brown. Stir in garlic and sauté for another 3 minutes, or until golden. Add ginger, asafoetida, cayenne, coriander, ajwain, ground cumin and salt, then stir well and sauté for 3 minutes. Stir in tomatoes and cook for 5 minutes, or until oil glistens on top. Stir in beef and water, reduce the heat to medium-low, cover and cook for 25 minutes.

Remove the lid and stir beef. (The beef should be cooking in its own juices and steam from the covered pot. However, if the beef or the masala is sticking to the bottom of the pan, stir in ⅔ cup more water.) Cover with the lid and simmer for 20 minutes more, or until tender.

Stir in rapini and cook, uncovered, for 3 to 4 minutes. Serve immediately.

Grilled Beef Tenderloin
with Almonds and Garlic

THIS tenderloin recipe goes with just about any curry. We find it easiest to marinate the beef in the morning and then cook our curry of choice in the evening.

Marinating the beef in the spices is important for a full, rich flavour. If you can't get any pomegranate powder, which is made from ground pomegranate seeds and better known as *anardana,* you can still make this dish—it just won't have that additional zing. Or use two tablespoons of tamarind paste instead of the pomegranate powder and this dish will have a bit more tartness to it. You can either pan-fry or grill the steaks in this recipe. We prefer our beef medium-rare, but you can cook your beef either less or more, according to your personal taste. Serve this dish with naan or slices of fresh baguette.

Beef marinade With a sharp knife, halve each tenderloin horizontally, as if you are going to make a sandwich. You should have 12 slices. In a large bowl, combine ⅓ cup of the oil, salt, cayenne, pomegranate powder (or tamarind paste) and paprika with the slices of tenderloin. Mix gently yet thoroughly with your hands until beef is well coated. Cover and refrigerate for at least 6 hours (the longer, the better).

Sautéed almond masala In a small frying pan, heat oil on medium-high for 1 minute. Add onion and sauté for 5 to 8 minutes, or until golden. Stir in garlic and sauté for 2 to 3 minutes, until light brown. Stir in almonds and sauté for 2 minutes, then remove from the heat and pour into a bowl or on to a plate. Allow to cool for at least 15 minutes.

Finish tenderloins To pan-sear beef, heat 2 tsp of the oil in a frying pan on medium-high for 1 minute. Place 2 slices of tenderloin in the pan and sear for 2 minutes. Gently turn over both steaks and sear for 2 minutes more. Transfer the cooked steaks to a plate. Sear the remaining steaks, adding 2 tsp more oil for each pair.

To grill the beef, heat the grill to high. Arrange the steaks loosely, in a single layer on the grill (you may need to grill them in batches) and, for medium-rare steaks, grill one side for 2½ minutes. Turn steaks over and grill for another 2½ minutes. If the steaks are not yet cooked or if you prefer them medium, grill each side for 1 minute more.

To serve, spread 1 Tbsp of the almond masala between 2 pieces of beef tenderloin.

SERVES 6

PREP & COOKING TIME
35 to 45 minutes + 6 hours or more to marinate the beef

Beef marinade

2½ lbs beef tenderloin (about 6 oz per serving), cut in 6 pieces

⅓ cup + 4 Tbsp cooking oil

1 Tbsp salt

1 tsp ground cayenne pepper

2 Tbsp pomegranate powder or tamarind paste (page 42, optional)

1 Tbsp paprika

Sautéed almond masala

¼ to ⅓ cup cooking oil

2 cups finely chopped onion (1 large)

1½ Tbsp finely chopped garlic (4 to 5 medium cloves)

½ cup chopped almonds (raw or roasted is fine)

SERVE WITH

Beet Greens Sautéed in Ginger, Lemon and Cumin

Rapini and Shiitake Mushroom Curry

Eggplant and Navy Beans in Kalonji and Tamarind Curry

Beef Short Ribs
in Light Cumin Broth

SHORT ribs are rich, velvety and, when cooked long enough, melt-in-your-mouth tender. You don't even need a knife to cut through the meat. The key is to let the short ribs simmer for about two hours on the stove or use a pressure cooker.

This atypical light broth complements the richness of the short ribs. It is also a very simple recipe, but it may take you a few tries to adapt the spices to your own preference. Remember that the spices are for flavouring the broth only. The Tomato and Onion Chutney (page 47) is also an excellent complement to the broth: just add a dollop per serving.

We make this recipe in a six-litre (six-quart) pressure cooker. Ours takes eleven minutes of pressure cooking, and we adjust the water to four cups. (If you have a smaller pressure cooker, reduce the beef to two pounds and the stock to between three and four cups, but keep the spice measurements the same.) Using stock gives this dish more depth, but you can also use water, especially if you are serving the chutney.

Serve this beef dish with white basmati rice or any rice pilaf that doesn't contain too much cumin.

In a small bowl, combine turmeric, cayenne, chili powder, salt and black pepper. Set aside.

Heat oil in a medium-large pot on medium-high for 1 minute. Sprinkle in cumin seeds and allow them to sizzle for 1 minute, or until dark brown but not black. Add the turmeric mixture and stir immediately. Stir for 20 seconds, then add short ribs and stock (or water). Stir and bring to a boil on high heat. Reduce the heat to low, cover and simmer for 2 to 3 hours, or until short ribs are very tender and the meat is easily pulled apart. Stir in cilantro and serve immediately.

SERVES 4 TO 6

PREP & COOKING TIME
10 minutes + 2 to 3 hours to simmer the short ribs

1 tsp turmeric

½ tsp ground cayenne pepper

2 tsp mild Mexican chili powder

1½ tsp salt

½ tsp black pepper (optional)

⅓ cup cooking oil

1 Tbsp cumin seeds

3 lbs boneless beef short ribs, cut in 2-inch x 3-inch pieces

5 cups stock (chicken, beef or vegetable) or water

¾ cup finely chopped cilantro

SERVE WITH

Beet Greens Sautéed in Ginger, Lemon and Cumin

Tangy and Spicy Chopped New Potatoes

Marinated Duck Breast with Mung Bean and Sesame Seed Rice Pilaf (without the duck)

‹ *shown here with Tomato and Onion Chutney, page 47*

Fennel and Kalonji–spiced Baby Back Ribs

SERVES 6 TO 8

PREP & COOKING TIME
1 hour + 5 minutes to grill or broil the ribs

Spice-infused ribs

3 lbs baby back ribs

10 cups water

6 whole dried cayenne peppers

½ tsp salt

10 cloves

3-inch cinnamon stick

VIKRAM was making a pork curry for dinner one evening when Meeru suggested that he serve a side dish with it. His idea of a side dish to the pork was more pork. After Meeru's initial shock, she realized the flavour of these ribs complemented the curry and we really enjoyed ourselves. The girls joked that after this pork feast they would pay dearly with vegetarian dinners for the next ten days.

Although we don't repeat this meal often at home, Vikram serves these back ribs with a pork tenderloin entrée at Vij's. His logic is that we treat ourselves when we go to a restaurant for dinner, and there's no point in holding back when you're treating yourself.

Baby back ribs, also called "loin ribs," are leaner and smaller than regular spare ribs. They do not come from baby pigs. Baby back ribs are taken from the top of the rib cage, which is closest to the backbone and the loin muscle. For lack of a better word, they are "daintier" than spare ribs and easier to eat, since most of the meat is on the top of the bone. In this recipe the ribs are double-spiced in that they are first boiled in whole spices and then rubbed with a spice mixture before being grilled or broiled.

Make the spice rub while the ribs are infusing. This recipe provides enough ground spices to make the rub for this dish three times. Be sure to store the leftover spices in an airtight container in a dark cupboard, where the mixture will keep fresh for up to three months. You can also freeze any leftover ribs in a resealable plastic bag or an airtight container and reheat them in a 375°F oven for ten to fifteen minutes, turning them halfway through.

Serve these ribs on their own as an hors d'oeuvre, as a side with seafood dishes or, as Vikram now does, as a "meat pickle" to accompany Meeru's vegetarian dinners. Of course, if you're treating yourself, you can serve these delicious ribs with any of the pork recipes in this book.

Spice-infused ribs Place back ribs, water, cayenne, salt, cloves and cinnamon in a large pot and bring to a boil on high heat. Cover, reduce the heat to medium and cook for 45 minutes. Using tongs, transfer ribs to a large bowl to cool. (If you want to save the infusion to use as a stock, allow it

continued overleaf...

2 Tbsp fennel seeds

12 green cardamom pods

16 cloves

½ tsp black peppercorns

1 tsp kalonji seeds

½ tsp ground mace

2 tsp ground
cayenne pepper

Spice rub

½ cup canned
crushed tomatoes

⅓ cup cooking oil

1 tsp salt

1 tsp finely chopped ginger

1 Tbsp ground spice mixture
(above)

SERVE WITH

Any recipe in this book,
but especially Pork Tenderloin
with Glazed Oranges

to cool slightly, then pour water through a sieve or colander into a clean airtight container and refrigerate for up to 7 days or freeze for up to 3 months. Discard any solids.)

Ground spice mixture Heat a small frying pan on high for 1 minute. Add fennel seeds, reduce the heat to medium-high and cook, stirring constantly, for 2 minutes (or less if you see the seeds turning brown). Transfer seeds to a small bowl and allow to cool for 15 minutes.

Combine fennel seeds, cardamom, cloves, peppercorns, kalonji, mace and cayenne in a spice (or coffee) grinder and process to obtain a powder. You should have 3½ to 4 Tbsp.

Spice rub To the bowl of ribs, add tomatoes, oil, salt, ginger and ground spice mixture. Wearing plastic gloves, mix well, rubbing the mixture into the meat so that tomatoes and spices fully cover the ribs.

Finish ribs Grilling is the best way to finish the ribs before serving, but if you're careful with the timing, you can also broil them.

To grill ribs, heat grill to high. Place ribs on the grill and cook for 2 minutes. Using tongs, turn ribs over and cook for another 2 minutes. Transfer to a serving platter.

To broil ribs, preheat the broiler. Arrange ribs on a baking sheet and broil for 2 minutes. Remove from the oven, and using tongs, turn ribs over and broil for another 2 minutes. Transfer to a large plate.

Fresh Fennel and Pork Curry

IN this recipe fresh fennel replaces onions. The fennel has a sweeter and milder flavour, so you need quite a bit more fennel than you would need onions. Although the recipe says finely chopped, the pieces will not be uniform in size. (Do not use the stalks of the fennel, as they are tough to chew.) We also use cubes of either pork shoulder or pork butt for this recipe. The pork shoulder is the top portion of the front legs, and the pork butt is from the upper shoulder, near the loin.

You can buy panch poran (page 21) at any Indian grocer. Although we don't use very much of it in this recipe, it adds a slightly pungent balance to the sweetness of the fennel. We also use a bit more salt here, but you can add your preferred amount. Serve the pork with chapatti or naan.

Heat oil in a medium pot on high for 1 minute. Add fennel and sauté, stirring regularly, for 15 minutes or until golden brown.

Add panch poran and asafoetida and sauté for 2 minutes, stirring regularly. The asafoetida may stick to the bottom of the pot. Add turmeric, coriander, cumin and salt and cook, stirring regularly, for 2 to 3 minutes. Stir in tomatoes and cook for 2 minutes, then reduce the heat to medium. Pour in balsamic vinegar and cook for 1 more minute. Turn off the heat.

To prevent buttermilk from curdling, place it in a small bowl. Stir 2 Tbsp of the masala into the buttermilk, then pour the mixture into the pot of curry and stir well. Turn on the heat to medium and sauté for 5 minutes, or until oil glistens on the masala.

Add pork, stirring well to completely coat it in the masala. Add water. Increase the heat to medium-high and bring to a boil, then reduce the heat to medium-low, stir well, cover and cook for 45 minutes. Stir the pork 2 or 3 times during that time. Cut off a small piece of pork and taste to see if it is fully cooked and tender (be careful, since it's hot). If pork is not cooked, add ½ cup more water, cover and cook for 15 minutes more. Turn off the heat and serve.

SERVES 6 TO 8

PREP & COOKING TIME
45 minutes + 1 hour to cook pork

½ cup cooking oil

3 ½ cups finely chopped fennel bulb (2 medium bulbs)

2 tsp ground panch poran (optional)

¼ tsp asafoetida

1 tsp turmeric

1 Tbsp ground coriander

2 Tbsp ground cumin

1 Tbsp + 1 tsp salt

1 cup puréed tomatoes (2 medium)

1 Tbsp balsamic vinegar (optional)

1½ cups buttermilk

3 lbs pork shoulder, trimmed of fat and cut in 2-inch dice

2 cups water

SERVE WITH

Roasted Eggplant Raita

Brown Basmati and Portobello Mushroom Pilaf

Paneer, Green Beans and Eggplant in Tamarind Curry

Pork Tenderloin

with Glazed Oranges

OUR business operations manager, Oguz (rhymes with froze) Istif, is from a small Turkish village near the Mediterranean Sea and he loves to talk about his mom's cooking. Every time he visits Turkey, he returns with photos of his mom's feasts. His stories and poetic descriptions are so vivid that we all have a mental image of what his mother and his home look like.

Meeru calls this her "Ode to Oguz" dish. Although all the spices are Indian (except for the sumac), this dish was inspired by Turkey. Our cultures use many of the same ingredients, especially nuts, dried fruits, beans and lentils. We find this connection reassuring, even though our cuisines are very distinct. When Meeru proudly served Oguz this dish, he smiled and calmly reminded her that he doesn't eat pork! For Oguz, Meeru replaced the pork with pheasant breast, and it was just as good.

If you don't eat pork, substitute grilled chicken or pheasant, as we did when we made this dish for Oguz. But if you do enjoy pork, stick with it in this recipe and you'll love it. We always serve it with the Spinach and Split Pea Mash (page 58) and topped with the Spiced Pistachios and Dates (page 60). Depending on your time and inclination, make just one of these parts or combine them all as we suggest here for a complete Indian meal with Turkish flavour. Whatever you decide, the glazed oranges are a bonus, not a necessity.

To serve this dish, place the curry; spinach and split pea mash; and pistachios and dates in separate bowls, then arrange them in the middle of the table along with a platter of tenderloin topped with the oranges so that guests can help themselves. (Let them know they should pour the curry over the other ingredients.) Alternatively, serve the tenderloin and oranges over bowls of rice or mash, top with cumin curry and garnish with pistachios and dates. For a quicker meal serve just the tenderloin and curry over rice.

....

Pork marinade In a large bowl, combine pork with ⅓ cup of the oil, salt, cayenne, paprika and garlic. Toss lightly with your hands to coat the pork, then cover and refrigerate for at least 3 hours.

continued overleaf...

SERVES 6

PREP & COOKING TIME
1½ hours + 3 hours
to marinate the pork

Pork marinade

2 ½ lbs pork tenderloin,
cut in 24 pieces and flesh
scored 1-inch deep

⅓ cup cooking oil +
¾ cup for searing

1 Tbsp salt

1 Tbsp ground
cayenne pepper

1 Tbsp paprika

1 Tbsp finely chopped
garlic (3 medium cloves)

Glazed oranges

1 Tbsp ghee or butter

5 cloves

1 tsp salt

¼ tsp ground cayenne pepper

3 Tbsp demerara sugar
or honey or other brown sugar

½ cup mango juice

1 large organic navel
orange, unpeeled,
sliced in ⅓-inch rounds

Cumin curry

½ cup cooking oil

2 Tbsp finely chopped
garlic (6 medium cloves)

½ cup all-purpose flour

½ Tbsp ground coriander

1 Tbsp ground cumin

½ Tbsp salt

1 Tbsp crushed cayenne pepper

6 cups stock (beef,
chicken or vegetable)

SERVE WITH

Spinach and Split Pea Mash and
Spiced Pistachios and Dates

Yam and Tomato Curry
(on the side)

Vegetable and Yellow Lentil
Curry (on the side)

Glazed oranges In a medium pot, melt ghee (or butter) on low heat and add cloves, salt, cayenne, sugar (or honey) and mango juice. Increase the heat to medium and bring to a light boil, stirring regularly. Add orange slices and stir gently but thoroughly. Bring to a light boil, cover, reduce the heat to low and simmer for 15 minutes. Remove from the heat and allow to cool. Will keep refrigerated, covered, for 2 to 3 days, but they will lose their texture when reheated.

Cumin curry Heat oil in a medium pot on medium-high for 45 seconds. Add garlic and sauté for 1 to 2 minutes, or until light golden. Stir in flour and cook, stirring regularly, for 4 minutes, or until flour is very light brown. Add coriander, cumin, salt and cayenne and sauté for 1 minute. Pour in stock, stir well until the curry is smooth, then reduce the heat to a simmer and boil gently for 5 minutes. Turn off the heat and set aside.

Finish pork Heat 2 Tbsp of the remaining oil in a frying pan on medium-high for 1 minute. Place 4 pieces of tenderloin in the frying pan and sear on one side for 2 minutes. Turn pork over and cook for 2 minutes. Transfer seared pieces to a clean plate or baking sheet. Repeat with the remaining pieces of pork.

When all of the tenderloin pieces have been seared, reheat cumin curry on medium-high for 4 to 5 minutes, or until hot. Serve immediately.

Spicy Pulled Pork Roast
with Garlic

THIS is a very simple and easy recipe, but the pork does take time to roast. Depending on our schedule, we sometimes roast it at 300°F for three hours (we find it's a bit juicer) or at 400°F for two hours to save time. We serve this dish like pulled pork, but if you are in a hurry, just serve the entire roast in its sauce and cut the slices at the table.

You will probably need to wear kitchen gloves while making this dish, as we use lots of garlic and spices. The pork absorbs and carries these spices well. Although the pork has enough fat of its own to cook the spices, adding the cooking oil to the dry spices cooks them with more finesse in the oven so that you don't risk getting a gritty texture. Remember that oven times vary, so check your pork for doneness carefully with a knife after 2 hours and adjust the cooking time accordingly.

This pulled pork is a heavier dish, so serve it with naan, baguette or any other bread of your choice. As with most curries, you can also serve it with rice. Or, make a Sloppy Joe–style sandwich.

Preheat the oven to 400°F.

Place pork in a roasting pan. In a large bowl, combine onion, garlic and oil. Add cumin, coriander, cloves, cinnamon, paprika, cayenne and salt and mix until well combined. Wearing plastic gloves, rub this spice mixture liberally all over pork. Don't worry if much of it falls off the pork and into the pan (obviously, the cinnamon stick will quickly fall off). Add water to the pan (do not pour it over pork), cover with foil and bake for 2 hours. Remove pork from the oven, cut off a small piece and taste it to be sure it is tender. If it is not, cover and return pork to the oven for up to 1 hour more. Remove pork from the oven and allow it to cool for 20 minutes, or until cool enough to touch.

Set the roasting pan beside a large bowl. Wearing plastic gloves, pull pieces of pork off the bones and place them in the bowl. Discard the bones, then add the pan juices to the meat and mix well.

SERVES 8 TO 10

PREP & COOKING TIME
40 minutes + 2 hours to roast

5 lbs pork shoulder (or pork butt)

2 cups chopped onion (1 large)

5 Tbsp finely chopped garlic (15 medium cloves)

⅓ cup cooking oil (optional)

4 Tbsp ground cumin

3 Tbsp ground coriander

10 cloves (optional)

2-inch cinnamon stick (optional)

2 Tbsp paprika (optional)

1 Tbsp ground cayenne pepper (optional)

1 Tbsp salt

2 cups water

SERVE WITH

Sour Cream Indian Dressing

Beet Greens Sautéed in Ginger, Lemon and Cumin

Red Bell Pepper, Onion and Sumac Sauté

Quinoa Salad with Lentil Sprouts

GOAT MEAT

Wherever meat is eaten in India, there is goat. When Indians want to make a fast meat curry, we use chicken. But a true meat curry is made with goat. Although it is considered a luxury meat in India, goat is not too popular in the European and North American cultures. We can't figure out why that's the case, except that goat takes time to cook and is usually served with the bone in. It may also be that goat doesn't come in any tenderloin or steak form.

According to Susan Schoenian, a sheep and goat specialist at the University of Maryland, goats are less likely to be confined (they don't do well), less likely to be fed any grain (it's not profitable), not implanted with growth promoters or fed antibiotics (it's not legal) and not castrated (ethnic buyers prefer intact males). Furthermore, goat meat has more iron and protein and much less cholesterol and saturated fats than other meats. Wes and Donna Gilmore of Painted River Farm, a cow and goat farm on Barnston Island in British Columbia, told us that any extra fat from food sources accumulates on a goat's lungs and heart and basically kills it. So, goats cannot be fattened quickly or unnaturally because when you try to feed them anything their bodies don't naturally take, they die. Goat meat, also known as chevon, is actually one of the cleanest, healthiest meats available.

We eat goat at home, and this year, Vikram spent time in Rajasthan, India, where he learned some new styles of cooking goat. Goat meat needs to be cooked in a heavy pot, with a good lid. Because it's lean, it needs to simmer longer than other meats to become tender: depending on the size and thickness of the pot, the oven temperature and the age of the goat, the meat can take anywhere from an hour and a half to three hours to stew. In our experience nine-month-old goats yield the ideal ratio of meat to tenderness.

(Younger goats yield less meat but take less time to cook than goats older than one year.)

Usually goat meat is sold bone-in and is cooked that way. The best cut is the leg, but shoulder and ribs, which are more bone and less meat, are also available. When you order goat meat from a butcher, be sure to request as much leg meat as possible. You can also ask for boneless goat meat, but since most people prefer to have the bones for stock, you may be hard pressed to find it. Most of the goat meat we buy in North America (and we go through *a lot* at our two restaurants) comes from New Zealand or Australia, because there has not been enough demand to support goat farmers in Canada and the U.S. (even though goats are not only a source of meat, milk and cheese; they also rid landscapes of unwanted weeds).

This past year we visited Wes and Donna on Barnston Island. The farm does not use any hormones or antibiotics on its animals or chemicals on its land. Although they raise the animals, the couple had never eaten goat meat. So we decided to take some goat curry to the farm and invite the Gilmores for a picnic. Nanaki made it very clear, however, that although she wanted to visit the farm and the goats, she would not eat goat meat in front of the goats. In the end we all agreed that doing this would be a bit uncomfortable, so we gave Donna, Wes and the goats' caretaker, Cassandra, some of Vikram's boneless goat curry (page 209) to eat on another occasion. For the picnic we went hypocritically vegetarian.

Our hope in including our goat meat recipes in the book is that we can entice you to try this delicious, healthy and versatile meat. At first glance all these recipes may look similar, but they are all subtly different in flavour and technique.

Simple Goat Curry

SERVES **6 TO 8**

PREP & COOKING TIME
2 to 2 ½ hours + 30 minutes
to take meat off bones

½ cup cooking oil

2 large onions, finely chopped

3 Tbsp finely chopped
garlic (9 medium cloves)

1 Tbsp finely chopped
ginger (optional)

2 Tbsp ground cumin

2 tsp ground coriander

1 tsp turmeric

2-inch cinnamon stick (optional)

1 tsp crushed cayenne pepper
or black pepper (optional)

1 Tbsp salt

3 lbs boneless goat leg
(or 6 lbs bone-in), cut in
1½- to 2-inch cubes

5 medium tomatoes
(about 1 ½ lbs), chopped

1 cup sour cream or plain
yogurt (minimum 2% milk fat),
stirred in 2 cups warm water

½ cup chopped fresh cilantro

PAINTED River Farm's goats are raised for the ethnic market, since that is where there is most demand. Chances are that you will find goat meat at your local Indian, Middle Eastern or Caribbean grocer, though your regular butcher may be able to source it for you. We recommend that, only if you have the time, you buy goat meat with the bone in and then take the meat off the bone once the curry is cooked. The bone adds flavour for a delicious broth in the curry, but boneless is also fine.

This is the recipe we usually make at home. Nanaki and Shanik prefer it, and there is little fuss in making it. For this recipe, use canned tomatoes in place of fresh if you can't find juicy fresh ones. You can also use half butter and half cooking oil, which will give you a richer-tasting curry. Similarly you can use sour cream instead of yogurt for a richer flavour. Serve this curry over white or brown basmati rice.

Heat oil in a large, heavy stockpot on medium-high for 1 minute. Add onions and sauté until slightly dark brown, 9 to 10 minutes. Add garlic and sauté for 2 to 3 minutes, until golden brown. (The onion will be dark brown but should not be black.) Stir in ginger, cumin, coriander, turmeric, cinnamon, cayenne (or black pepper) and salt and cook on medium heat, stirring regularly, for 3 to 5 minutes, or until oil separates from the onion-spice mixture. (Add another tsp of oil or ghee if spices are sticking to the bottom of the pot.)

Add goat meat, stir well and sauté for 3 to 4 minutes. Reduce the heat to medium, then stir in tomatoes and cook for 3 to 4 minutes, stirring regularly. Pour in the sour cream (or yogurt)-water mixture, stir well, then increase the heat to medium-high and bring to a boil. Reduce the heat to medium-low and cover with a heavy lid. Simmer for 30 minutes, then remove the lid and stir. The meat should be simmering in the soup. If there is not enough liquid, add one more cup of water, replace the lid and continue cooking.

After goat has stewed for 1¼ hours, remove a piece from the pot, allow it cool for a minute and taste it to see if it is tender. If it is done, remove from the heat. If not, cook the goat meat, covered, for another 30 to 45 minutes. Once goat meat is cooked, turn off the heat. (As long as there is still liquid in the pot, do not worry about overcooking the goat; it just becomes more tender.)

If you have cooked goat with the bones in but want to serve it boneless, allow it to cool for 20 minutes. Wearing plastic gloves, pull the meat off the bones. Discard the bones and return the goat meat to the curry. Just before serving, heat the curry on medium-high for 10 minutes, or until it begins to boil. Mix in cilantro and serve immediately, piping hot.

SERVE WITH

Celery, Tomato and Green Onion Sauté

Spicy Cauliflower "Steak"

Punjabi Lentil Curry (for dinner parties)

Meeru's Oven-braised Goat Curry

SERVES 8

PREP & COOKING TIME
2 ½ to 3 hours
(including baking time)

½ cup cooking oil

2 cups finely chopped
onion (1 large)

3 Tbsp finely chopped
garlic (9 medium cloves)

3 cups puréed tomatoes
(6 medium, or canned is fine)

½ cup tomato paste

3 Tbsp ground cumin

2 Tbsp ground coriander

1 tsp ground
fenugreek seeds

1 tsp turmeric

1 ½ tsp ground cayenne
pepper (optional)

3-inch cinnamon
stick (optional)

1 Tbsp salt

3 lbs boneless goat meat
(or 6 lbs bone-in), cut in
1 ½- to 2-inch dice

6 cups warm water

1 ½ cups sour cream or
whipping cream

1 ½ Tbsp dried green
fenugreek leaves (optional)

THE first time Meeru visited Painted River Farm, all the goats came up to her and started "goat talking." They nudged her, stood as close to her as possible, sucked on her hands and purse and jeans (they don't have top teeth, so no damage), and even jumped on her. Their affection was great, and it reminded Meeru of India.

Meeru began to visit India regularly when she was twenty-one. Unlike in North America, where many guests have come to expect their own room, when Meeru stayed with family members or her parents' friends in India, she often shared a bed with a cousin (or two) or a family's child. This common practice led to lots of late-night "bed talking," open conversations in which her bedmates asked frank questions and shared just as much information about themselves. Their attitude was as loving and as social as the goats'.

Cassandra, Painted River's goat caretaker, explained that even when she puts the farm's goats in the truck to take them to the abattoir, they smile and readily enter the vehicle as if they are going to attend a party. Although she finds it hard to lead them to slaughter (especially since she has given all the goats names), Cassandra believes that eating meat is a natural part of life and she takes pride in knowing that her goats led a comfortable and healthy life and that they were slaughtered ethically. We have heard similar comments from other meat farmers at our local farmers' market.

For this dish you will need a large heavy ovenproof casserole dish with a tight-fitting lid. The goat curry takes about two hours to braise in the oven, which gives you plenty of time to do other things. Serve this dish with bowls of rice and/or pieces of naan.

Preheat the oven to 400°F.

Heat oil in a medium-large pot on medium-high for 45 seconds. Add onion and sauté until browned, 7 to 8 minutes. Stir in garlic and sauté for 2 minutes, or until brown. Add tomatoes and tomato paste, stir well, then add cumin, coriander, fenugreek seeds, turmeric, cayenne, cinnamon and salt. Stir and sauté for 5 to 8 minutes. Turn off the heat and add the water and sour cream (or whipping cream). Stir well.

Place goat meat in a large ovenproof dish, carefully add the tomato-spice-cream mixture and mix until well combined. Braise the goat curry in the oven for 1 hour.

Remove the curry from the oven, uncover and stir. The curry should be fairly soup-like. If it is not, add 1 more cup of water. Replace the lid and oven-braise the curry for 1 more hour, or until goat meat is tender and cooked. Remove from the oven, stir in fenugreek leaves and serve.

For a boneless curry, wait until the goat meat is cool enough to handle, about 20 minutes. Wearing plastic gloves, peel the meat from the bones. Discard the bones, and return the goat meat to the curry. Stir well to combine.

SERVE WITH

Brown Basmati and
Portobello Mushroom Pilaf

Mushroom and Celery Root
Basmati Rice Pilaf

Indian-style Tomato,
Onion and Paneer Bruschetta
(for dinner parties)

Vikram's Boneless Goat Curry

VIKRAM loves to spend a Sunday afternoon luxuriously chopping, mixing and getting just about every dish and spoon in the kitchen dirty. The girls will linger and help out, but Meeru stays away because the sight of the dirty dishes piling up and the mess in the kitchen make her nervous. This curry is definitely worth the mess, though, and if you can't dine at Vij's, you most likely won't get it elsewhere.

Make the bone-in goat curry (page 211) one day as well, and decide for yourself which recipe you prefer. We serve this curry with white or brown basmati rice or naan.

Stewed goat In a large pot on medium-high heat, combine ghee (or butter), salt, goat meat and water. Stir regularly for 10 to 15 minutes, or until meat is browned and begins to release its juices. Cover and reduce the heat to low, then cook for 1¼ hours, stirring every 15 minutes. The goat meat and bones will release water and should not stick to the bottom of the pan. If the meat is sticking, add ½ to 1 cup more water.

While the goat meat is stewing, make the masala in a separate pan.

Masala In a large pot, heat oil on medium-high for 1 minute. Add cumin seeds, cloves, cinnamon and black cardamom, stir and allow cumin seeds to sizzle for 30 seconds. Stir in onion and sauté for 7 to 8 minutes, or until crispy brown on the edges.

Add garlic and sauté for 2 minutes, or until browned. Stir in ginger, tomatoes, black pepper, ground cumin, garam masala, turmeric, salt, paprika and cayenne. Reduce the heat to medium, cover and cook for 3 minutes.

Place yogurt in a small bowl. To prevent curdling, spoon 2 to 3 Tbsp of the hot masala into the yogurt. Stir well, then pour the yogurt mixture into the pot of masala. Sauté masala for another 2 minutes, then stir in water, increase the heat to high and bring to a boil. Cover, reduce the heat to low and simmer for 10 minutes. Turn off the heat.

continued overleaf...

continued overleaf...

SERVES 6

PREP & COOKING TIME
2 ½ hours

Stewed goat

½ cup ghee or butter

1 tsp salt

6 lbs goat meat, bone-in, cut in 1½- to 2-inch dice

1 cup water

Masala

½ cup cooking oil

1 Tbsp + 1 tsp cumin seeds

10 cloves

3-inch cinnamon stick

5 black cardamom pods, lightly pounded (optional)

1 lb red onion, thinly sliced

3 Tbsp chopped garlic (9 medium cloves)

2 Tbsp finely chopped ginger

3 cups puréed tomatoes (6 medium)

1 tsp black pepper

2 Tbsp ground cumin

2 Tbsp garam masala (page 41)

1 tsp turmeric

1½ tsp salt

1 Tbsp paprika (optional)

1½ tsp ground cayenne pepper (optional)

1 cup plain yogurt (minimum 2% milk fat), stirred

6 cups water

Finish curry After goat has stewed for 1¼ hours, remove a piece from the pot, allow it cool for a minute and pull some meat off the bone. If it pulls off easily and is tender, remove the pot from the heat. If not, cook the goat meat for another 15 minutes. Once goat meat is cooked, turn off the heat and allow to cool for 20 to 30 minutes.

Set the pot of cooled goat meat beside the pot of curry. Wearing plastic gloves, pull the goat meat off the bones. Discard the bones and return the goat meat to the pot of curry.

Just before serving, heat goat curry on medium-high and bring it to a boil. Stir and reduce the heat to medium, cover and simmer for 10 minutes. Serve immediately.

Vikram's Bone-in Goat Curry

DURING his recent visit to Rajasthan, Vikram spent a few nights visiting Thakur Pritvi Singh of Kanota at his palace. The Thakur's cook prepared many dishes for Vikram, and this recipe was partly inspired by that experience. Both Meeru and Vikram grew up eating goat curry with the bones in, and Vikram loves to make this dish for friends as a surprise. He acts as if eating the meat off goat bones is an everyday occurrence, and it's fun to see people follow his lead and start picking up pieces of goat meat with their fingers and sucking the tender meat off the bones. Even though this dish is eaten with your hands, it really isn't that messy, especially if you serve it with naan or rice to soak up some of the rich curry broth.

Heat ghee (or oil) in a large pot on medium-high for 1 minute. Add cumin seeds, cinnamon, cardamom and cloves and allow cumin seeds to sizzle for 30 seconds. Stir in onions and sauté for 7 to 8 minutes, or until crispy brown on the edges.

Stir in goat meat and salt, then cook, stirring regularly, for 10 minutes. (The meat will release some of it juices during this time.) Reduce the heat to medium, cover and cook for 35 minutes, stirring occasionally. (You may need to add ½ cup of water if the meat is sticking to the pan.)

Add garlic and ginger and stir well, then add tomatoes and water, cover and continue cooking for 1 hour.

In a large bowl, combine black pepper, nutmeg, coriander, turmeric, paprika, cayenne and yogurt. To prevent the yogurt from curdling, stir 3 or 4 Tbsp of the hot curry into the yogurt. Pour the yogurt into the pot of curry and stir well. Cover and cook the meat for another 20 to 45 minutes, or until goat is tender and cooked. Remove from the heat and serve.

SERVES 6 TO 8

PREP & COOKING TIME
2 to 2 ½ hours

½ cup ghee or cooking oil

1 Tbsp + 1 tsp cumin seeds

3-inch cinnamon stick

5 black cardamom pods, lightly pounded (optional)

10 cloves

1 lb red onions, thinly sliced

6 lbs goat meat, bone-in, cut in 1½- to 2-inch dice

1 Tbsp salt

3 Tbsp chopped garlic (9 medium cloves)

2 Tbsp finely chopped ginger

4 cups puréed tomatoes (8 medium)

7 cups water

1 tsp black pepper

2 tsp nutmeg

2 Tbsp ground coriander

1 tsp turmeric

1 Tbsp paprika (optional)

2 tsp ground cayenne pepper (optional)

2 cups plain yogurt (minimum 2% milk fat), room temperature, stirred

SERVE WITH

Eggplant and Paneer Pâté (for dinner parties)

Punjabi Lentil Curry (this is a rich combination)

Vegetable and Yellow Lentil Curry

211

DESSERTS

VIKRAM DOESN'T EAT much dessert because he's decided that he prefers his sugar from wine and he doesn't have the luxury of not having to watch his weight. But he does love Indian desserts in concept—the more traditional and the sweeter, the better. Meeru, Nanaki and Shanik find most Indian desserts too sweet or too oily, so coming up with recipes for Indian desserts is a difficult job. The three of them are chocolate lovers, and they're increasingly finding that chocolate lovers aren't always good partners for Indian desserts.

The four desserts in the following pages are family favourites. By this we mean that Meeru, Nanaki and Shanik enjoy them immensely and Vikram will have the occasional taste. The vast majority of Indian desserts are dairy based, but we do have one dairy-free recipe here. Nanaki's favourites are the coconut fruit pudding and the tapioca. We serve the coconut fruit pudding at Rangoli, where it's a staff favourite as well. Shanik loves the chickpea flour pudding (the name doesn't sound appealing, but you'll have to trust us). If you like nutty-tasty, wintry desserts (without the nuts), you'll enjoy this one. When we have the time, the entire family—including Vikram, who will eat bowls of this—enjoys the carrot halwa. Carrot halwa is the Indian version of carrot cake, minus any flour.

When making Indian desserts, try to use Indian raw sugar (*gur*) or Latin American *panela*, which looks like brown sugar but tastes more like maple or date sugar. The exception is in the coconut pudding, a very light dessert that is easily overpowered by the heavier sugar.

Home Grow-in Old-fashioned
Indian Carrot Halwa

SERVES 8 TO 10

PREP & COOKING TIME
4 hours

5 lbs carrots, washed and
grated (peeled is optional)

1 gallon whole milk

10 to 15 green cardamom pods,
lightly pounded (optional)

2½ cups demerara
sugar or Indian raw sugar

1½ Tbsp raw sugar (optional)

1 cup whipping cream,
whipped (optional)

IN the spring of 2009 Deborah Reynolds (known to everyone as Deb) suddenly showed up in our neighbourhood and opened a tiny grocery store called Home Grow-in, in what seems like a garage. It turns out that the place was a general store in the 1940s, and Deborah was able to renew those permits to open her own shop. Deborah sells milk, poultry and eggs, breads, fruits and vegetables, and other specialty food items made and grown only by local artisans and farmers. (In March 2010 Deborah received the Order of Canada for facilitating the transfer of 160,000 pounds of organic products—that would otherwise have rotted or been composted—from local farms to local food banks.) For kids she sells ice cream for a dollar a mini-cone and a child-sized bag of caramel popcorn for eighty-nine cents. She always gives the kids an apple, chocolates or peaches as "samples" to take home.

One Saturday afternoon, we took Nanaki, Shanik and their friends to Home Grow-in for some ice cream. We also picked up some chicken and other items but didn't have enough cash to pay for them, so Meeru took out her credit card. Shanik whispered that Deborah doesn't take credit cards. She was worried about having already eaten the ice cream but not being able to pay for it. When Meeru asked, "You don't take credit cards?" Deborah whipped back, "No, but I'll take trust" and handed Meeru the receipt. It took Shanik a few seconds, but she broke out in a smile when she understood.

On our way out Deborah handed us ten pounds of eggplant and some bell peppers grown by a local farmer, saying, "Try that. If you like it, Carmen [the farmer] will drop off whatever you need for your restaurants every Monday at my shop." When we returned to Home Grow-in to give Deborah a sample of the eggplant raita (page 50) we'd made with the produce, we saw beautiful carrots, clumped with dirt and looking as if they had just been picked from the farm. We bought five pounds for five dollars and immediately thought about making carrot halwa. This dessert is similar to rice pudding but made with carrots instead of rice, and the milk is cooked much longer, so it has a more intense flavour. Today many Indian cooks use shortcuts such as whipping cream, sweetened condensed milk and/or dried milk to reduce the cooking time. But if you go to Amritsar or another Punjabi city, a real *halwai*, or traditional sweet-maker, will make carrot halwa the old-fashioned way, which is still the best. Because of the amount of time it takes to make it, we don't have carrot halwa on any of our menus, and we make it at home only for a special occasion or if the girls beg for it. This recipe makes the old-fashioned, Punjabi halwai-style carrot halwa that we made with Deborah's fresh carrots.

If you really want to make an Indian happy, serve one of the goat meat curries followed by this carrot halwa for dessert! Be sure to serve the halwa warm.

In a large pot, combine carrots, milk and cardamom and bring to a boil, stirring regularly, on medium-high heat. Reduce the heat to medium and continue cooking, uncovered, for 2 hours, stirring every 10 to 15 minutes. As the milk condenses into the carrots, you will have to stir more vigorously and scrape milk off the sides of the pan. It will be a whitish yellowy-orange. (The milk should be boiling but not burning in the pot; if you are scraping brown-coloured milk from the sides of the pan, turn down the heat.)

Add demerara (or raw) sugar and stir thoroughly. Cook for another ¹/₂ hour, or until milk has condensed into the carrots. The halwa is ready when the milk dries up and the carrots glisten. We serve the halwa with the cardamom pods, but remove them if you like.

Although it is optional, we highly recommend that, in a small bowl, you fold the 1¹/₂ Tbsp of sugar into the whipped cream and serve a dollop over each serving.

Indian raw sugar

Indian Raw Sugar and Ginger Tapioca

SERVES 8 TO 10

PREP & COOKING TIME
30 minutes to soak tapioca
+ 25 minutes to cook it

1 cup pearl tapioca

2 cups water

4 cups whole milk

1 cup whipping cream

8 oz raw sugar

½ tsp finely chopped ginger

WHILE walking home from school one day, Shanik asked, "Mom, have you heard of Cool Whip?"

"Yeah, I have," Meeru answered.

Pause. "So why didn't you ever tell me about it!?"

"Because you'll get addicted to the fake stuff and not like real whipped cream."

"But, Mom, I eat potato chips and I love real potatoes!"

Despite her protests, Shanik wasn't getting anywhere with Meeru. It turned out that her friend Stella had never tried Cool Whip either, and they were determined to taste it—all of the other girls on the playground were shocked that they didn't know what Cool Whip was.

A few days later, on their walk home from school with Stella's dad, Gordon, the girls casually went into the corner grocer, found the Cool Whip and asked, "Hey, can we try this stuff?"

"But that's Cool Whip!" Gordon replied.

"Please, Daddy?"

Gordon bought the Cool Whip on the condition that the girls eat it with some strawberries. They went to Stella's house and had a Cool Whip picnic. When Shanik came home that night, she told Meeru and Vikram that she was going to explode from eating too much Cool Whip.

Meeru smiled, remembering that her mom used to make this tapioca recipe below, using only milk, and Meeru would top it with tons of Cool Whip. Now we add a cup of real whipping cream to the recipe. It's not sophisticated, but you can't get more satisfying than this dessert.

Use the Indian raw sugar, known as *gur*, which you can buy at any Indian grocer, or *panela*, the Latin American raw sugar; otherwise there is nothing extra special about this tapioca. We like the ginger mild, but the finer you chop the ginger, the better the flavour. Add an extra quarter teaspoon if you like a stronger taste.

Tapioca is difficult to reheat, so you'll have to eat any leftovers cold or ignore the lumpy texture if you prefer to eat it warm. Alternatively, you can use a half cup (instead of one cup) tapioca and reduce the water to one cup, and you will have a "soupier" dessert that won't clump as much.

Combine tapioca and water in a medium bowl and soak for 30 minutes. Drain water. In a medium pot, combine tapioca, milk, cream, sugar and ginger, then heat on medium-high (or medium if you have a high-powered, hot stove) and bring to a boil, stirring often. Reduce the heat to a simmer and continue to stir and cook tapioca for 15 to 20 minutes, or until thick like pudding.

Coconut Pudding
with Fresh Fruits

WITHOUT the Rooh Afza, this coconut pudding would taste like many other Asian versions. An Indian-Pakistani grenadine, Rooh Afza is a very pretty bright magenta and has a distinct, rose-like flavour that is inexplicable until you taste it. In Urdu, *rooh* means "soul" and *afza* means "nourishment." The drink was developed in Delhi by Hakeem Hafiz Abdul Majeed in 1907 as a sweet and refreshing herbal tonic. (*Hakeem* is the word for a herbal medicine doctor, and going to a hakeem is very common in India.) It is also meant to give energy, which is why it is a popular drink during Ramadan. Before commercial soda pop was widely available, Indians kept a bottle of Rooh Afza in the cupboard, mixing it into a drink with water or milk and ice for guests.

Although we're not sure if the recipe has changed, it was originally composed of pineapple, watermelon, orange and carrot extracts, plus some medicinal herbs and sugar. Now made in both India and Pakistan by Hakeem Abdul's company Hamdard Laboratories, Rooh Afza is very sweet, so you don't need to add very much. In addition to its use in drinks, Rooh Afza is added to many desserts, and we like to mix a little into fruity cocktails. You can buy it at any Indian grocer in North America. Add whichever fruits you like to this pudding, or eat it on its own without the fruit. Serve this dessert chilled.

In a medium heavy-bottomed saucepan, combine coconut milk and rice flour. Bring to a boil on medium heat, then reduce the heat to low, stir and cook for 5 minutes. Stir in sugar, cook for 1 minute, then turn off the heat and allow to cool for 10 minutes. Stir in Rooh Afza.

Scrape pudding into a bowl, cover and refrigerate until serving. Top with fruits right before serving.

SERVES 6 TO 8

PREP & COOKING TIME
15 minutes (+ time to cut fruits)

6 cups coconut milk, stirred

2 Tbsp rice flour

¾ cup white sugar

4 Tbsp Rooh Afza

1 to 1½ cups chopped fruits, such as fresh berries; green or red grapes, halved and seeded; mango, in small pieces; tangerines, clementines or satsuma oranges, peeled and cut in small pieces; plums, chopped; canned lychee, drained and chopped; bananas, sliced; kiwi, chopped

Sweet Chickpea Flour Pudding
with Almonds

PREP & COOKING TIME
35 minutes with almonds
(or 25 minutes without)

1½ oz (36) raw
almonds (optional)

½ cup unsalted butter

¾ cup chickpea flour

5 cups milk (whole or 2%)

1 cup demerara sugar
or Indian raw sugar

THIS pudding—minus the almonds—is Shanik and Meeru's favourite after-school snack or "Indian dessert." Although we're not sure about the origins of this pudding, which is usually eaten for breakfast almost like oatmeal, it must be a rustic peasant food, as we have never seen it served to guests or even outside of anyone's home. We tend to forget how much butter and sugar go into this sweet dish because we focus on the chickpea flour and milk. Chickpea flour is high in protein, iron and fibre and is very healthy, and milk is obviously of great value to the Indian diet.

This pudding is basically like making a béchamel sauce. Stirring with a whisk is crucial to the outcome, so be sure to have one handy when you make this pudding. As well, the higher the quality of the sugar you use, the better this dessert will taste. We've used raw Indian sugar, date sugar and demerara sugar, but you can use plain white sugar if that's all you have.

We add six roasted almonds per serving, but if you're an almond lover, add as many of the nuts as you like. You can mix them into the pudding or sprinkle them on top. Just remember that if you double the number of almonds, you may need to add an extra tablespoon of sugar to the pudding. If you don't like almonds, eat this pudding on its own.

Note that, like other milk-based puddings, this one will form a thin skin on top as it cools. Simply stir the pudding with a whisk and reheat it before serving any leftovers.

Place almonds in a small, heavy-bottomed frying pan over medium heat. Stir regularly and cook for 2 minutes. You may get a few small black patches on some of the almonds; that's fine, you won't taste them. Turn off the heat and spread almonds on a plate to cool for 10 to 15 minutes.

While almonds are cooling, make the pudding. In a medium pot, melt butter on low heat. Add chickpea flour, stir well with a whisk and increase the heat to medium. Keep stirring, completely blending the flour into the butter. Cook, stirring regularly, for 8 to 10 minutes, or until the flour darkens. (This means the chickpea flour is completely cooked.)

Keeping your head away from the pot, gently pour in milk. (The milk will sizzle when it first touches the hot batter.) Stir well with the whisk. Stir in sugar, bring to a boil, then reduce the heat to low. Cook for 10 minutes while stirring regularly with a whisk. Turn off the heat.

Roughly chop the almonds and sprinkle over the pudding.

METRIC CONVERSION CHART
rounded off to the nearest whole number

WEIGHT

IMPERIAL OR U.S.	METRIC
1 oz	30 g
2 oz	60 g
3 oz	85 g
4 oz	115 g
5 oz	140 g
6 oz	170 g
7 oz	200 g
8 oz (½ lb)	225 g
9 oz	255 g
10 oz	285 g
11 oz	310 g
12 oz	340 g
13 oz	370 g
14 oz	400 g
15 oz	425 g
16 oz (1 lb)	455 g
2 lbs	910 g

VOLUME

IMPERIAL OR U.S.	METRIC
⅛ tsp	0.5 mL
¼ tsp	1 mL
½ tsp	2.5 mL
¾ tsp	4 mL
1 tsp	5 mL
1 Tbsp	15 mL
1½ Tbsp	23 mL
⅛ cup	30 mL
¼ cup	60 mL
⅓ cup	80 mL
½ cup	120 mL
⅔ cup	160 mL
¾ cup	180 mL
1 cup	240 mL

TEMPERATURE

IMPERIAL OR U.S.	METRIC
250°F	120°C
275°F	135°C
300°F	150°C
325°F	160°C
350°F	180°C
375°F	190°C
400°F	205°C
425°F	220°C
450°F	230°C
475°F	245°C

INDEX